SPOOKY
HALLOWEEN
CRAFTS

by Susan Cousineau

NORTH LIGHT BOOKS
CINCINNATI, OHIO
www.artistsnetwork.com

About the Author

Susan Cousineau is a freelance designer and author living with her husband, Tom, and their very spoiled pets, in the picturesque town of Fort Frances, Ontario.

In addition to Susan's first book with North Light Books, *Easy Christmas Crafts*, she has authored twelve previous booklets and has contributed to ten multidesigner books since the start of her professional design career over a decade ago. Several of Susan's designs have also been published by national craft magazines and have appeared on numerous book and magazine covers. Susan has an honors degree in business administration and a diploma in computer graphic design.

For Susan, what makes Halloween so special is the time spent with family and friends on a night when anything goes! The crazy costumes, the dreadful decor, the terrible tricks and tasty treats . . . what fun it is for kids of all ages to celebrate the spooky magic of this haunted holiday. Susan hopes all the frightfully fun ideas in this book will inspire you to make your next Halloween simply "terror-ific." Happy haunting!

METRIC CONVERSION CHART

TO CONVERT	TO	MULTIPLY BY
Inches	Centimeters	2.54
Centimeters	Inches	0.4
Feet	Centimeters	30.5
Centimeters	Feet	0.03
Yards	Meters	0.9
Meters	Yards	1.1
Sq. Inches	Sq. Centimeters	6.45
Sq. Centimeters	Sq. Inches	0.16
Sq. Feet	Sq. Meters	0.09
Sq. Meters	Sq. Feet	10.8
Sq. Yards	Sq. Meters	0.8
Sq. Meters	Sq. Yards	1.2
Pounds	Kilograms	0.45
Kilograms	Pounds	2.2
Ounces	Grams	28.3
Grams	Ounces	0.035

Spooky Halloween Crafts. Copyright © 2004 by Susan Cousineau. Manufactured in China. All rights reserved. The patterns and drawings in the book are for the personal use of the reader. By permission of the author and publisher, they may be either hand-traced or photocopied to make single copies, but under no circumstances may they be resold or republished. It is permissible for the purchaser to make the projects contained herein and sell them at fairs, bazaars and craft shows. No other part of this book may be reproduced in any form or by any electronic or mechanical means including information storage and retrieval systems without permission in writing from the publisher, except by a reviewer, who may quote a brief passage in review. Published by North Light Books, an imprint of F+W Publications, Inc., 4700 East Galbraith Road, Cincinnati, Ohio 45236. (800) 289-0963. First edition.

08 07 06 05 04   5 4 3 2 1

Library of Congress Cataloging-in-Publication Data
Cousineau, Susan.
    Spooky Halloween crafts / by Susan Cousineau.
        p. cm.
Includes index.
ISBN 1-58180-447-4 (pb. : alk. paper)
1. Halloween decorations. 2. Handicraft. I. Title.

TT900.H32C69 2004
745.594'1646--dc22
                                                    2003055787

Editor: Jolie Lamping Roth
Designer: Marissa Bowers
Layout Artist: Kathy Gardner
Production Coordinator: Sara Dumford
Photographers: Christine Polomsky and Al Parrish
Photo Stylist: Mary Barnes Clark

Dedication

This book is dedicated to all of my frightfully fiendish family and friends who have given me so many wacky and wonderful Halloween memories over the years.

From the wicked warlocks, to the horrible hags and blood-thirsty vampires, you're what makes this spooky occasion so terribly terrific!

I wish all of you grown-up ghouls many more happy Halloween nights full of thrills and chills, horrifying haunts and lots of spooky surprises.

Acknowledgments

Special thanks to my family, especially my husband, Tom, Pops and Laurie, Auntie Mary, and Michael and Karen, for your continued encouragement and support.

I would also like to express my sincere thanks to North Light Books for another wonderful opportunity and to the very talented crew of ghostly ghouls who made this book a reality: Tricia Waddell, for giving me the chance to share all of my creepy creations; my editor, Jolie Lamping Roth, for all of her guidance and hard work; Christine Polomsky, for taking such beautiful pictures and for making the photoshoot so frightfully fun; and Marissa Bowers, for her "spook-tacular" book design. It has been a pleasure working with all of you.

My heartfelt thanks also goes out to all the companies who so generously provided the supplies for this book: Creative Paperclay Company (Michael Gerbasi), Delta Technical Coatings, Inc. (Barbara Carson), Loew-Cornell, Inc. (Shirley Miller), Duncan Enterprises (Linda Bagby), and Activa Products, Inc. (Vickie Kay).

When I'm not riding my broom, I'm usually hanging out with all of my creepy critters.

My brother and me one frightful night, many, many moons ago.

My evil twin "Hagatha" and her dreadful date are ready for a spooky night on the town!

Table of Contents

Tools & Materials 6

Painting Terms & Techniques 8

Pick A Treat!

R.I.P.

SECTION

1

HAUNTED HIDEAWAY 10

Ghost Decoration.......................................12

Haunted House 14

Jingle Bell Pumpkin...................................18

Scared Stiff Ghost Topiary 20

Hideaway Quick Crafts 24

    Broom Hilda

    Ghost Gift Bag

    Fluttering Friend

    Mr. Bones Pot

SECTION 2

FRIGHTFULLY FUN FAVORS & GIFTS 26

Mummy Spoon 28

Black Cat Candy Cup 30

Mummy Can 33

Pumpkin Pin Pal 34

Frightfully Fun Quick Crafts.................36

   Scaredy Cat Munchie Mix Bags

   Going Buggy Sucker Bouquets

   Frankie Favor Cup

   Mr. Whiskers Peat Pot

SECTION 3

Quick & Eerie Edibles 51

   Creepy Caramel Apples

   Monster Munchie Hand

   Scaredy Cat Cupcakes

   Cookie Monster Pizza

   Crispy Corn Mummy Balls

   Yummy Bat Droppings

MONSTER MASH 38

Pick-A-Treat Jar 40

Severed Fingers 42

Haunted Graveyard Stage.........................44

Cookie Monster Pizza Box 47

Monster Quick Crafts 48

   Ghost Finger Puppet

   Ghost Messenger Party Invitations

   Scary Skull Ornament

   Spooky Spider

Terror-ific Tips 50

Using Patterns & Templates 54

Patterns...55

Resources 62

Index 63

Tools & Materials

Here's a brief introduction to some of the basic supplies you will need to create the projects in this book. For a complete listing of the supplies required for each project, please refer to the individual project instructions.

Loew-Cornell Brushes

Below is a list of the brushes used to create the projects in this book.

- Series 410: ⅛-inch (3mm), ¼-inch (6mm) and ⅜-inch (10mm) deerfoot stippler brushes. (Use the deerfoot stipplers to drybrush cheeks. The brush size will depend on the size of the cheek area for each project. These brushes are also used to stipple Broom Hilda's hair [see page 24] and to apply texture and shading to various projects. You can also use old "fluffy" brushes of various sizes for the drybrush and stippling techniques.)
- American Painter Series 4000: nos. 3 and 5 round brushes
- American Painter Series 4300: nos. 4, 6 and 8 shader (flat) brushes
- American Painter Series 4350: 10/0 and no. 0 liner brush (for painting fine details and delicate lines)
- American Painter Series 4550: ¾-inch (19mm) wash brush (great for basecoating large areas)

PAINTBRUSHES

General Painting Supplies

In addition to the brushes, you will need a few general painting materials.

- Delta Ceramcoat acrylic paints (refer to individual project instructions for suggested colors)
- Delta Ceramcoat matte interior varnish (brush-on)
- Delta Ceramcoat matte interior spray varnish
- Old toothbrush (for projects that are spattered)
- Brush basin or water tub (to rinse brushes)
- Paper towels
- Palette or wax paper

DIMENSIONAL AND ACRYLIC PAINTS

Miscellaneous Supplies

The projects in this book require a number of miscellaneous supplies. Some of the more readily available supplies, such as a ruler, pencil or scissors, are mentioned here, but they are not mentioned in the projects' materials lists. Skim through each project's instructions before beginning to make sure you have everything within reach.

- Ruler, sharp knife and scissors
- Glue gun and glue sticks
- Tacky glue
- Blow-dryer (to speed up the drying process)
- Tulip (or Scribbles) dimensional paints (refer to individual project instructions for required colors)
- Iridescent crystal glitter
- Small pieces of sponge (I use the compressed sponge sheets that expand in water)
- Fabric stiffener
- Fine-point black permanent marker (such as the Pigma Micron 05 or Zig Memory System 05)
- Foam brush (for applying fabric stiffener onto cheesecloth)

Transferring Patterns

The following are materials you will need to transfer the patterns on pages 55–61. If you do not wish to transfer the patterns, use them as a guide and freehand the details. For directions on transferring patterns and creating templates, see page 54.

- Transparent tracing paper
- Gray transfer paper (or use white transfer paper for projects that have a dark background)
- Pencil and eraser (optional: ballpoint pen)
- Lightweight cardboard or posterboard (if making templates)

INSTANT PAPIER MÂCHÉ

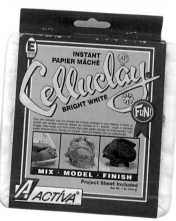

AIR-DRY MODELING CLAY

Plaster Gauze

Nothing could be easier than creating "spook-tacular" Halloween decorations using an instant plaster gauze. I use Activa's Rigid Wrap Plaster Cloth. Simply cut your desired pieces of plaster cloth, moisten in water and voila! They're ready to apply onto your base form. With a little creepy creativity, you'd be surprised at how regular household items can become enchanting decorating delights. An empty milk carton is transformed into a spooky haunted house (see page 14), and a coffee can plays the role of a mummy treat container (see page 33) . . . it's so quick and easy!

Instant Papier Mâché

Celluclay Instant Papier Mâché is a great alternative to traditional papier mâché techniques. There are no strips of newspapers to cut or messy paste required. You simply mix the prepackaged paper pulp with water in a mixing bowl and you have an "instant" papier mâché mixture to work with.

In this book, the papier mâché mixture is applied onto Styrofoam ball shapes to make delightful Halloween candy cups (see pages 30–32). However, feel free to let your imagination run wild as you create all sorts of spooky papier mâché characters. A papier mâché-covered Styrofoam cone would make the perfect witch, or use a variety of ball and egg shapes to make a perky pumpkin patch and a frightful family of bats or spiders. The possibilities are endless!

Air-Dry Modeling Clays

Creative Paperclay and Delight modeling compound are two wonderful brands of air-dry clays that are extremely pliable and great for creating projects with a smooth, lightweight finish. Crayola Model Magic in white is another brand that works great for the Severed Fingers and Ghost Finger Puppet projects. Creative Paperclay can be easily flattened with a rolling pin, just like cookie dough. Once rolled, you can press your favorite cookie cutter shapes into the flattened Paperclay to make delightful ornaments and trims.

AIR-DRY CLAY TIPS

- Cover your work surface with wax paper or plastic wrap to prevent clay from sticking.
- While working on your project, keep excess clay in a resealable plastic bag to prevent dryness.
- For even drying, turn your projects over repeatedly to allow the air to circulate.
- Use a small heater or blow-dryer to speed up drying.
- Keep a bowl of warm water handy to clean and moisten your fingers. If using cookie cutters to form clay shapes, dip them into the water first to prevent the clay from sticking.
- Use hand lotion to prevent dryness while sculpting with clay.

Painting Terms & Techniques

Below is a list of painting terms and techniques used throughout this book. I've even included some tips on page 9 to make creating your easy Halloween crafts even easier!

Basecoating

Using a flat brush, apply at least two coats of paint to ensure solid coverage. Be sure to allow the paint to dry in between coats. If you like, you can use a blow-dryer to speed up the drying process.

Stippling and Drybrushing

The stippling technique is used to texture the Haunted House (see page 16) and Broom Hilda's hair. (See art below. For complete project instructions, see page 24.) With a touch of paint on a deerfoot or old "fluffy" brush, gently pounce the bristles up and down to apply the desired texture.

For drybrushing, use a deerfoot brush or an old "fluffy" brush and dip the bristles in a small dab of paint. Remove most of the paint from the brush on a dry paper towel. You basically want a "dry brush" with just a hint of color. Gently rub the bristles on the surface area until you have achieved the desired effect. This technique is a great way to apply softly colored cheeks to your projects and to apply subtle texture and shading (see art below).

Spattering or "Fly Specking"

For this technique, use an old toothbrush to apply tiny specks of paint to the surface area. Although some designers prefer to thin their paint with water first (approximately $2/3$ paint to $1/3$ water), I prefer to simply moisten the toothbrush bristles, then dip the toothbrush into a pool of paint. Remove excess paint onto a paper towel, then run your finger across the ends of the bristles, holding the toothbrush over the area to be spattered (see art below).

Wash

Thin a small dab of paint with water to achieve a transparent color. Apply the wash to your surface, gradually adding more coats to deepen the color to the desired shade. This technique is commonly used to shade and antique projects.

Dots and Highlights

The easiest way to make dots is to dip the end of a paintbrush handle into a fresh dab of paint, then apply the tip to your surface. Repeat this process for

STIPPLING

To stipple, use a deerfoot brush or an old "fluffy" brush with just a touch of paint and gently pounce the bristles up and down to add texture.

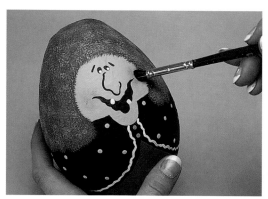

DRYBRUSHING

To drybrush the cheek areas of your project, first remove most of the paint from the brush using a dry paper towel. With only a hint of color on the brush, gently rub the bristles on the surface area.

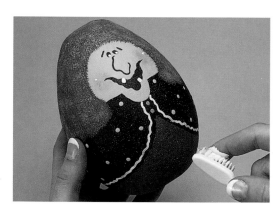

SPATTERING

For the spattering technique, moisten the toothbrush bristles, dip the toothbrush into a pool of paint, then remove excess paint onto a paper towel. Next, hold the toothbrush over the area to be spattered and run your finger across the ends of the bristles.

each dot needed. You can vary your dot sizes by using a smaller or larger paintbrush handle. For tiny highlight dots, however, I recommend using the bristle-end of a regular liner brush.

Sponge Painting

Several projects have been painted using small pieces of sponge. (I use the sheets of compressed sponges that expand when moistened in water.) It's important to remember that all painting should be done with a damp, not wet, sponge, so be sure to squeeze the excess water from the sponge. If your sponge is too wet, the paint will bleed on your surface.

This sponge-painting technique can be used in many ways. For example, it can be used to apply a basecoat color to a project, create a textured effect or create a geometric design. The size of the sponge you will cut will depend on the size of the area to be painted. You simply dip the dampened sponge into a pool of paint and apply it onto the surface of your project. When basecoating, you can apply additional coats as necessary to achieve solid coverage. Remember when cutting your sponge pieces that they will expand slightly when moistened in water.

PAINTING TIPS

GENERAL:
- Before attempting any new painting technique, always practice first on a spare piece of paper.
- Cover your work surface with wax paper. Wax paper makes a cost-effective palette for your painting and sponge-painting techniques.
- Use a blow-dryer to speed up the drying process.
- Have a brush basin or container of clean water handy to rinse your brushes. Don't allow the paint to dry on the bristles.

STIPPLING:
- If you apply too much paint during the stippling process, simply reverse or subdue the effect by stippling with the base color.

SPATTERING:
- I always test the spatters before applying this technique (or do the backside of the project first just to be safe).
- The more water you add to your paint or to the bristles of your toothbrush, the larger and more transparent your spatters will be.

BASECOATING USING SPONGE PAINTING
A sponge can be used to basecoat large areas, like the Cookie Monster Pizza Box shown here (see page 47 for complete project instructions).

TEXTURIZING USING SPONGE PAINTING
Use a sponge to add texture and definition to areas of a project. Here I am creating a stone texture for the base of the Scared Stiff Ghost Topiary (see pages 20–23 for complete project instructions).

HAUNTED
HIDEAWAY

READY TO SET THE STAGE FOR SOME SPOOKY FUN?

It's Halloween . . . the perfect time to transform your "home sweet haunted home" into a house of horrors, full of creepy crafts, terrifying trims and delightfully dreadful decorations. If you dare to enter our Haunted Hideaway, you'll discover an enchanting collection of frightfully fun decorating delights that even your grown-up ghosts and ghouls are sure to approve of.

Cast an eerie spell on your trick-or-treaters with a charming witch egg, then scare them silly with a terrifying topiary ghost—the perfect centerpiece for a frightful Halloween feast. And remember to hang on to those empty milk cartons; they make delightful haunted houses for your friendly spirits to inhabit. On the not-so-scary side, there's a jolly jingle bell pumpkin decoration and a "boo-tiful" paper bag ghost that will warm your heart on even the chilliest of Halloween nights.

Once you've decked your haunted halls with these creepy creations, you'll be ready to celebrate your ghostly gatherings in "spook-tacular" style!

SECTION

1

GHOST DECORATION 12

HAUNTED HOUSE 14

JINGLE BELL PUMPKIN 18

SCARED STIFF
GHOST TOPIARY 20

HIDEAWAY
QUICK CRAFTS 24

GHOST Decoration

Don't get spooked . . . this friendly ghost is just hanging around to join in some Halloween fun. Crafted from brown kraft paper, he's simply charming with his bat eraser buttons and homespun raffia bows. For a great gift idea, package your ghostly spirit in a coordinating tote bag made from the same simple shape (see page 24).

MATERIALS LIST

- paintbrushes and general supplies (see pages 6–7)

- tracing paper and transfer paper

- kraft paper (such as heavy brown paper bags or parcel wrap)

- polyester fiberfill

- Delta Ceramcoat acrylic paint: Light Ivory, Charcoal, Hippo Grey, Cardinal Red (for a softer look, use pink powdered blush for the cheeks instead of Cardinal Red)

- Tulip Pearl Snow White (or Scribbles Iridescent White Mist) dimensional paint

- Delta Ceramcoat matte interior spray varnish

- 36" (91cm) general-purpose wire

- $3/8$" (1cm) wooden dowel

- three strands orange raffia

- two strands black raffia

- $1/2$"–$5/8$" (1cm–2cm) orange button

- three miniature bat erasers (or plastic bats) for buttons

- wire cutters (optional)

- old toothbrush

- glue gun and glue sticks

- pattern (page 55)

PROJECT TIP

If you are making several Ghost Decorations, see the instructions on page 54 to create a ghost template.

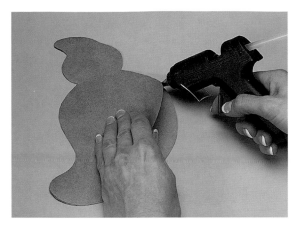

1 Trace two ghost shapes (see pattern on page 55) onto kraft paper and cut out. (See page 54 for instructions on transferring patterns.) Line up the edges of the two ghosts. Hot glue the inside edges together, leaving an opening large enough at the bottom to stuff the fiberfill once the ghost is painted.

2 Basecoat the ghost Light Ivory and let dry. Next, paint the facial features (freehand the features or transfer the pattern on page 55) using Charcoal for the eyes and eyebrows, Light Ivory for the pupils and Hippo Grey for the nose. Add a Light Ivory highlight dot to the nose. Then add a Charcoal squiggly line down the center of the nose.

For the cheeks, either drybrush with Cardinal Red or brush on pink powdered blush. Add Light Ivory highlight dots. Using an old toothbrush, spatter the ghost with Charcoal.

4 For the wire hanger, use sharp scissors or wire cutters to cut a 36" (91cm) piece of general-purpose wire. Curl the wire by wrapping it tightly around a ³/₈" (1cm) wooden dowel. Insert the ends of the wire hanger through each side of the ghost and twist the ends to secure.

3 Use the white dimensional paint to accent the edges of the ghost, and allow to dry. Then apply the matte spray varnish and let dry.

Stuff the ghost with small pieces of fiberfill. Use the tip of a pencil or paintbrush handle to push the fiberfill into hard-to-reach areas. Hot glue the remaining edges shut.

5 Tie a bow onto the top of the wire hanger using three strands of orange and two strands of black raffia. Hot glue the bow at the back to secure.

Next, hot glue the orange button onto the center of the raffia bow. Then hot glue the three miniature bat erasers down the front of the ghost for buttons.

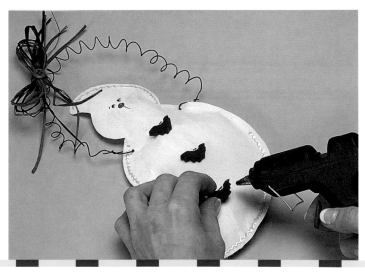

HAUNTED House

You can almost hear the creaky doors, rattling chains and eerie shrieks coming from this spooky mansion. But not to fear . . . the friendly spirits that haunt this milk carton house are anything but scary. To add some frightful fun to your creepy creation, embellish your haunted hangout with charming bats, ghosts, pumpkins and cats crafted from air-dry clay and miniature cookie cutters. For a final touch, hang a spooky clay skeleton bone over the door to scare away any unwanted guests.

MATERIALS LIST

- paintbrushes and general supplies (see pages 6–7)
- ½ gallon (2L) milk carton
- plaster gauze (I use one standard size 180" x 4"[5m x 10cm] wide roll of Rigid Wrap Plaster Cloth)
- air-dry modeling clay (I use Creative Paperclay)
- white acrylic gesso
- Delta Ceramcoat acrylic paint: Palomino Tan, Charcoal, Hippo Grey, Light Ivory, Terra Cotta, Dark Forest Green
- Delta Ceramcoat matte interior spray varnish
- miniature Halloween cookie cutters (I use a ghost, pumpkin, bat, cat and dog bone)
- masking tape
- wax paper
- rolling pin
- bowl of warm water
- old toothbrush
- glue gun and glue sticks
- patterns (page 55)

Create a Haunted Scene

Create a gruesome graveyard setting for your haunted house with spooky black trees, autumn leaves, Spanish moss and artificial spider webbing. Craft tombstones out of Styrofoam pieces and fleckstone paint, and create a rickety picket fence from broken craft sticks or twigs. For the final touch, visit a novelty or party supply store to purchase miniature skeletons, ghosts, bats and ghouls that can haunt your spooky scene. You can even make an entire haunted Halloween village by using various sizes of milk cartons.

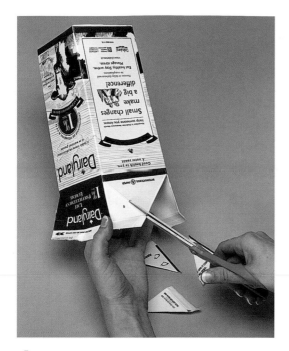

2 Fold the edges over to form the rooftop and secure the top and sides with masking tape.

1 Open the top of the empty milk carton. Wash the inside and allow to dry. Next, cut the two outer pieces from each side along the folds. You will be left with a triangular shape on the top of each side.

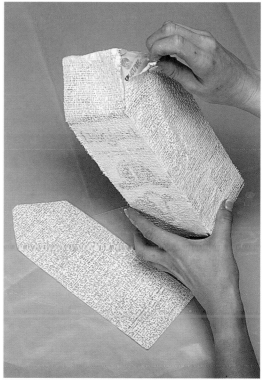

3 Cover your work surface with wax paper. For the front and bottom, cut one 15" (38cm) piece of plaster gauze. (Note: Milk cartons may vary in size, so be sure to measure the carton you are using before cutting. A standard size roll of Rigid Wrap is 4" [10cm] wide, which should be the right width to cover the carton.) Following the manufacturer's instructions, moisten the piece of gauze in water, then apply it onto the carton, smoothing the surface with your fingers. For the back, cut one 11" (28cm) piece. Moisten, then apply the piece, smoothing the surface area. Use your fingers to smooth the seams where the front and back pieces meet.

4 For the sides, cut two 10" (25cm) pieces of gauze. Then cut the plaster gauze in a triangular shape at the top of each piece to follow the peak of the rooftop. Moisten the side pieces and apply, making sure to line up the triangular top to fit the shape of the rooftop. Use your fingers to smooth the seams at each corner of the house where the four pieces meet.

Repeat steps 3 and 4, adding two more layers of plaster gauze. (I recommend applying a total of three layers to make the house extra sturdy.) Allow to dry. Then apply a generous coat of white acrylic gesso to seal the surface of the house. Apply additional coats if desired and allow to dry.

5 Basecoat the house Palomino Tan and the rooftop Charcoal. Randomly stipple the house with Hippo Grey for added dimension and texture. Add more stippling at the corners for contrast.

6 For the front and sides of the house (steps 6–8), freehand or trace the door and window patterns (see page 55) as instructed. For the left side of the house, paint two windows with Charcoal. Trim the windows and paint the window boxes with Hippo Grey. In each corner of the window boxes, add tiny Charcoal dots for the nails. With Light Ivory, paint a spider web in the bottom window. In the top window, paint spooky eyes using Light Ivory with Charcoal for the pupils.

7 For the front of the house, paint a door using Hippo Grey with Charcoal trim. Use Charcoal and a liner brush to outline the planks. Add tiny Charcoal dots for the nails.

Paint the window Charcoal with Hippo Grey trim and a Hippo Grey window box. Again, paint tiny Charcoal dots in each corner of the window box for the nails. Paint a spider web in the window using Light Ivory.

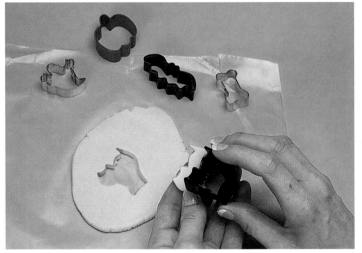

8 For the right side of the house, paint a window using Charcoal. Trim the window and paint a window box using Hippo Grey. In each corner of the window box add tiny Charcoal dots for the nails. Paint spooky eyes in the window using Light Ivory. Use Charcoal for the pupils. Use an old toothbrush to spatter the house with Light Ivory. Then apply the matte spray varnish.

9 To make the house ornaments, cover your work surface with a clean piece of wax paper. Use a rolling pin to flatten the air-dry modeling clay to a ¹/₄" (6mm) thickness. Cut out bone, cat, pumpkin, ghost and bat shapes using miniature cookie cutters. For my house, I made one bone, one cat, three pumpkins, six ghosts and five bats.

Next, dip your fingers in a bowl of warm water to moisten, then blend the edges of the clay ornaments until smooth. (You can also use the bowl of warm water to clean and moisten your cookie cutters to prevent the clay from sticking.) Allow the clay ornaments to dry. Be sure to turn them over frequently to allow even drying.

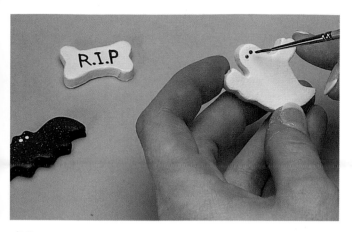

10 Paint the bat, bone and ghost ornaments. Use Charcoal for the bats and add eyes using Light Ivory. Paint the bone Light Ivory and write "R.I.P." using Charcoal. Paint the ghosts Light Ivory. Use Charcoal for the eyes.

11 For the cat ornament, basecoat it with Charcoal. Paint the eyes Light Ivory and add Charcoal for the pupils. Paint the nose and inside of the ears Terra Cotta. Use Light Ivory for the whiskers, mouth and the line between the legs.

12 Basecoat the pumpkins Terra Cotta. Then blend some Terra Cotta paint with a tiny drop of Charcoal to form a brownish color. Use a mixture of Terra Cotta and the brownish color to shade the ridges on the pumpkin. Paint the stem Dark Forest Green. Add three tiny highlight dots to the right side of the pumpkin using Light Ivory.

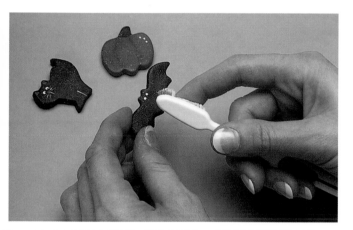

13 Use an old toothbrush to spatter the cat, bat and pumpkin ornaments with Light Ivory. Then apply the matte spray varnish to all of the ornaments.

14 Hot glue the ornaments onto the haunted house as desired.

Make Spooky Pins

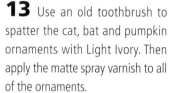

These house ornaments make great Halloween pins. See the Pumpkin Pin Pal project on pages 34–35 for instructions.

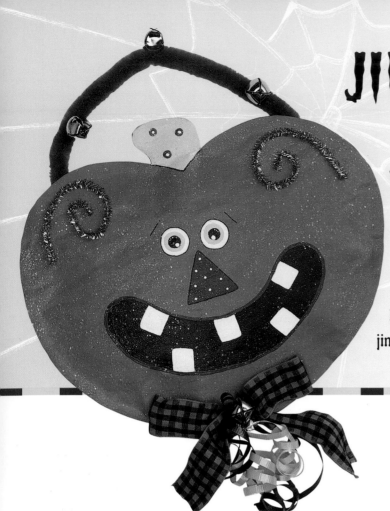

JINGLE BELL
Pumpkin

Welcome your trick-or-treaters and ghostly guests with this jolly jingle bell pumpkin decoration. Grinning from ear to ear, this perky pal is the pick of the patch and will surely brighten the spooky spirits in your haunted hallways! Crafted from brown paper bags, he's simply charming with his homespun bow and jingle bell trims. What a fun way to "ring in" the Halloween season.

PROJECT TIP

If you are making more than one Jingle Bell Pumpkin, see the instructions on page 54 to create a pumpkin template.

MATERIALS LIST

- paintbrushes and general supplies (see pages 6–7)

- tracing paper and transfer paper

- kraft paper (such as heavy brown paper bags or parcel wrap)

- polyester fiberfill

- Delta Ceramcoat acrylic paint: Bittersweet Orange, Lima Green, Deep Lilac, Charcoal, Light Ivory

- Delta Ceramcoat matte interior spray varnish

- iridescent crystal glitter

- DecoArt Glamour Dust

- two 6" (15cm) pieces of 6mm silver tinsel stems

- 12" (30cm) 15mm purple chenille stem

- four 16mm silver jingle bells

- 18" (46cm) of 1" (3cm) wide orange and black plaid ribbon

- purple, white and lime green curling ribbon

- fine-point black permanent marker (such as the Pigma Micron 05 or Zig Memory System 05)

- old toothbrush

- glue gun and glue sticks

- pattern (page 56)

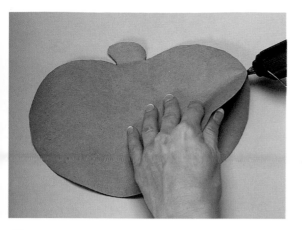

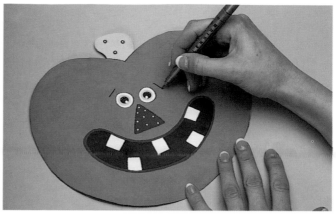

1 Trace two pumpkin shapes (see pattern on page 56) onto kraft paper and cut out. (See page 54 for instructions on transferring patterns.) Line up the edges of the two pumpkins. Hot glue the inside edges together, leaving an opening large enough at the bottom to stuff the fiberfill once the pumpkin is painted.

2 Basecoat the pumpkin Bittersweet Orange and the stem Lima Green, and let dry. Next, paint the facial features (freehand the features or transfer the pattern on page 56). The eyes are three painted circles beginning with Light Ivory, Lima Green, then Charcoal. Use Light Ivory to add the pupils and three tiny highlight dots. Paint the nose Deep Lilac with Light Ivory dots. For the mouth use Charcoal, and for the teeth use Light Ivory.

Next, outline the edge of the mouth with Deep Lilac. Add three Deep Lilac dots to the stem and paint a Light Ivory center dot on each. To finish, outline the eyes, nose, stem and eyebrows using a black permanent marker.

4 Cut two 6" (15cm) pieces of silver tinsel stems. Twist each stem into a spiral shape and hot glue onto the top sides of the pumpkin.

For the hanger, hot glue the purple chenille stem onto the back of the pumpkin. Hot glue three silver jingle bells onto the hanger.

3 Using an old toothbrush, spatter the pumpkin with Light Ivory, and let dry. Apply the matte spray varnish. While the varnish is still wet, sprinkle with iridescent crystal glitter and Glamour Dust.

Stuff the paper bag pumpkin with small pieces of fiberfill. Use the tip of a pencil or paintbrush handle to push the fiberfill into hard-to-reach areas. Hot glue the remaining edges shut.

5 Cut an 18" (46cm) piece of orange and black plaid ribbon and tie into a bow. Trim the ends of the bow to the desired length. Hot glue a silver jingle bell onto the center of the bow. Tie purple, white and lime green curling ribbon around the jingle bell for a festive touch. Hot glue the bow onto the bottom of the pumpkin.

SCARED STIFF
Ghost Topiary

This ghostly greeter has risen from the grave to haunt your home with Halloween cheer. Rising from his clay pot tombstone, this fiendish fellow rattles his rusty chain as he wanders through the pumpkin patch. With his Styrofoam egg body and stiffened cheesecloth robe, it's easier than you think to bring this graveyard ghoul back to life!

MATERIALS LIST

- paintbrushes and general supplies (see pages 6–7)
- 4¼" (11cm) clay pot
- floral foam brick
- 6" (15cm) Styrofoam egg
- two 6" (15cm) pieces of general-purpose wire
- six 18" x 2" (46cm x 5cm) wide strips of cheesecloth
- three 18" x 15" (46cm x 38cm) wide pieces of cheesecloth
- 9" (23cm) wooden dowel, ⁵⁄₁₆" (8mm) diameter
- fabric stiffener (I use Aleene's Fabric Stiffener & Draping Liquid)
- white acrylic gesso
- Delta Ceramcoat acrylic paint: Lichen Grey, Charcoal, Light Ivory, Cardinal Red (for a softer look, use pink powdered blush for the cheeks instead of Cardinal Red)
- Delta Ceramcoat matte interior varnish

- iridescent crystal glitter
- Spanish moss
- 18" (46cm) chain link
- miniature plastic bat
- two miniature raffia pumpkins (I use one 1" [3cm] and one 1½" [4cm])
- artificial spider webbing
- small piece of sponge
- sharp knife
- wire cutters (optional)
- wax paper
- plastic container or bowl (for fabric stiffener)
- 2" (5cm) foam brush
- 1" (3cm) miniature clothespins
- old toothbrush
- glue gun and glue sticks
- patterns (page 56)

PROJECT TIP

Use your ghostly greeter to light up the night by using glow-in-the-dark paints or accenting with a miniature set of battery-operated Halloween lights.

1 Using a dampened piece of sponge, apply Lichen Grey to the surface of the pot. Then, very sparingly, sponge paint with Charcoal then Light Ivory to give a stone-textured look to the tombstone pot.

2 Paint the letters "R.I.P." (see pattern on page 56) using Light Ivory with Charcoal shadows. Using an old toothbrush, spatter the pot with Light Ivory and let dry.

Apply the matte varnish to the pot. While the varnish is still wet, sprinkle the pot with iridescent glitter.

3 Using a sharp knife, cut the floral foam brick to fit the inside of the pot. Hot glue to secure and let set.

4 To form the arms, use sharp scissors or wire cutters to cut two 6" (15cm) pieces of general-purpose wire. Bend each piece in half to form a loop shape, then twist the ends together. Insert the ends of the wire loops into the sides of the Styrofoam egg for the arms. Hot glue to secure.

5 Cut six strips of cheesecloth approximately 18" x 2" (46cm x 5cm) wide. Wrap three strips of cheesecloth around each wire loop arm to build up to the desired thickness. Hot glue to secure.

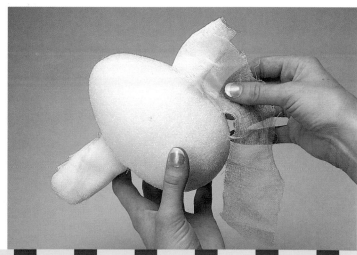

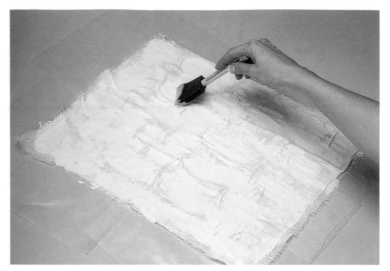

6 Use the sharp knife to cut a 9" (23cm) length of the ⁵/₁₆" (8mm) wooden dowel. Insert one end of the dowel into the bottom of the Styrofoam egg approximately 2" (5cm) deep. Remove the dowel, then apply hot glue into the hole. Reinsert the dowel and allow the glue to set.

Next, insert the other end of the dowel into the center of the floral foam base approximately 2" (5cm) deep. Remove the dowel, then apply hot glue into the hole. Reinsert the dowel and allow the glue to set.

7 Cut three pieces of cheesecloth approximately 18" x 15" (46cm x 38cm) wide. You may want to cut each cheesecloth layer slightly larger to account for subtle variations in the arm and dowel lengths. To be on the safe side, test the size first by draping the cloth over the ghost armature shape.

Next, stack the three layers directly on top of one another. Then set the cheesecloth layers on wax paper. Pour the fabric stiffener into a plastic bowl. Use a foam brush to apply the liquid onto the cheesecloth layers until well saturated.

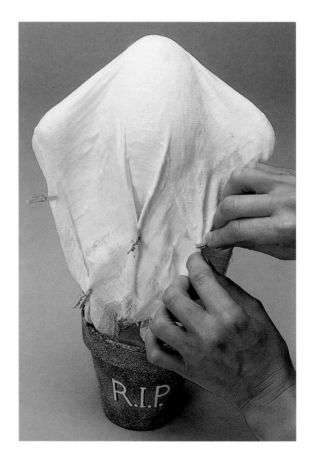

8 Drape the three layers of cloth over the ghost armature and continue to apply the fabric stiffener as necessary to ensure the cloth is moistened thoroughly. Use the miniature clothespins to secure the side openings. Shape as desired, using the miniature clothespins to hold the creases and folds for added dimension. **Note: Allow to dry, but be sure to remove the clothespins as soon as the cloth begins to harden. If you leave the clothespins on until the ghost is completely dry, it will be very difficult to remove them.**

Apply a generous coat of white acrylic gesso to seal the surface of the ghost. Apply additional coats of gesso if desired. Allow to dry.

9 Basecoat the ghost Light Ivory and let dry. Next, paint the facial features. Simply freehand or trace them by referring to the pattern on page 56. Paint the eyes Charcoal with Light Ivory pupils and the mouth Charcoal with a Light Ivory highlight. For the cheeks, either drybrush with Cardinal Red or brush on pink powdered blush. Apply the matte varnish to the ghost, and while the varnish is still wet, sprinkle the ghost with iridescent glitter.

10 To decorate the topiary, hot glue the Spanish moss onto the base of the pot and around the front area of the ghost. Next, hot glue the chain link onto the arms of the ghost. Glue the miniature plastic bat onto one end of the chain link. Then hot glue the two miniature raffia pumpkins onto the base of the pot.

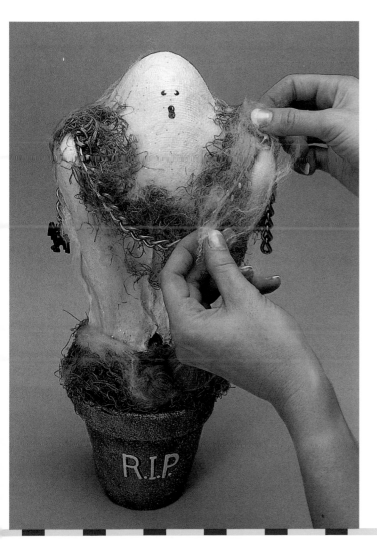

11 Drape the artificial spider webbing onto the ghost and around the base of the pot. Hot glue the webbing to the base of the pot if desired.

Scared Stiff
Centerpiece

For a chilling centerpiece, set the ghostly greeter on your haunted Halloween table surrounded by spooky black trees, artificial spider webbing and colorful autumn leaves. Complete your ghostly theme with the Ghost Finger Puppet favors and Ghost Messenger Party Invitations featured on page 48.

HIDEAWAY QUICK CRAFTS

Broom Hilda

MATERIALS: paintbrushes and general supplies (see pages 6–7) / 6" (15cm) papier mâché egg / Delta Ceramcoat acrylic paint: Lima Green, Charcoal, Hippo Grey, Lichen Grey, Light Ivory, Terra Cotta, Cardinal Red / Delta Ceramcoat matte interior spray varnish / 3½" x 4" (9cm x 10cm) black felt witch hat / one strand orange raffia / 4" (10cm) miniature broom / artificial spider webbing / old toothbrush / glue gun and glue sticks / pattern (page 56)

1 Firmly press the bottom of the egg onto a hard surface so it sits upright. Trace or freehand the main basecoat areas: face, hair, dress and cape (see pattern on page 56). **2** Paint the face Lima Green, the cape Charcoal, the dress Terra Cotta, and the hair Hippo Grey. For texture, stipple the ends of the hair with Hippo Grey. Next, stipple the hair with Lichen Grey, and, when dry, very sparingly stipple with Light Ivory. Paint the details onto the cape using Light Ivory for the trim, Lima Green for the dots and Lichen Grey for the buttons, and let dry. **3** Trace or freehand the facial features (see pattern on page 56). Paint the mouth, eyes, nose and eyebrows Charcoal. Use Light Ivory for the teeth and pupils. For the cheeks, drybrush with Cardinal Red and use Light Ivory for the highlight dots. **4** Use an old toothbrush to spatter the witch with Light Ivory, then apply the matte spray varnish. When dry, hot glue a hat to the top of the head, a raffia bow to the hat and a broom to the witch. Drape artificial spider webbing around the witch and hot glue the ends to the bottom of the egg to secure.

Ghost Gift Bag

MATERIALS: paintbrushes and general supplies (see pages 6–7) / tracing paper and transfer paper / white posterboard / orange gift bag / Delta Ceramcoat acrylic paint: Light Ivory, Charcoal, Hippo Grey, Cardinal Red / white and black dimensional paint / spray varnish / three miniature bat erasers (or plastic bats) / black and orange raffia / ½"–⅝" (1cm–2cm) orange button / old toothbrush / tacky glue / glue gun and glue sticks / pattern (page 57)

1 Trace the ghost pattern (see page 57) onto white posterboard and cut it out. **2** Paint and decorate the ghost referring to the Ghost Decoration instructions on pages 12–13. Then glue the ghost to the gift bag using tacky glue. **3** Add black dimensional paint dots around the ghost, then spatter the bag with Light Ivory and Charcoal. Let dry. For the finishing touch, hot glue a black and orange raffia bow and an orange button to the bottom of the handle.

Fluttering Friend

MATERIALS: paintbrushes and general supplies (see pages 6–7) / tracing paper and transfer paper / 4" (10cm) or 5" (13cm) papier mâché egg / black posterboard / Delta Ceramcoat acrylic paint: Charcoal, Lichen Grey, Light Ivory, Wild Rose / Delta Ceramcoat matte interior spray varnish / $\frac{1}{8}$" (3mm) hole punch / $\frac{3}{8}$" (1cm) wooden dowel / 36" (91cm) 20-gauge silver wire / wire cutters (optional) / old toothbrush / glue gun and glue sticks / patterns (page 57)

1 Basecoat the egg with Charcoal. Trace or freehand the facial features (see pattern on page 57). Paint the eyes Light Ivory with Charcoal pupils, the nose Wild Rose with a Light Ivory highlight dot, the mouth Lichen Grey, and the fangs and freckles Light Ivory. Next, outline the ears with Lichen Grey. Paint the inside of the ears Wild Rose and add Light Ivory highlight dots. **2** Using an old toothbrush, spatter the bat with Lichen Grey. Apply the matte spray varnish. **3** Trace the wing shape (see pattern on page 57) onto black posterboard and cut out. Spatter the wings with Lichen Grey. Apply the matte spray varnish. **4** Hot glue the wings onto the back of the bat egg. Use a hole punch to insert a hole into the top center of each wing. For a hanger, curl a 36" (91cm) piece of wire around a wooden dowel. Then insert each end of the wire through the holes in the wings and twist the ends to secure.

Mr. Bones Pot

MATERIALS: paintbrushes and general supplies (see pages 6–7) / 4" (10cm) wide rose pot, 5$\frac{1}{2}$" (14cm) high / Delta Ceramcoat acrylic paint: Light Ivory, Charcoal, Lima Green, Deep Lilac, Dark Goldenrod / Delta Ceramcoat matte interior spray varnish / 2" (5cm) and $\frac{5}{8}$"–$\frac{3}{4}$" (1.5cm–1.9cm) square pieces of sponge / fine-point silver metallic paint marker / patterns (page 57)

1 Use a 2" (5cm) piece of dampened sponge to apply Light Ivory onto the base of the pot. Next, use the sponge to apply Deep Lilac onto the rim of the pot. Allow to dry. Use a $\frac{5}{8}$"–$\frac{3}{4}$" (1.5cm–1.9cm) square piece of sponge to apply Dark Goldenrod checks onto the rim. **2** When dry, add a Lima Green dot onto the center of each Dark Goldenrod check. Use a silver metallic paint marker to draw a circle around each dot. **3** Trace or freehand the facial features (see pattern on page 57). Paint the eyes Charcoal with a Lima Green iris and a Charcoal pupil. The highlight dot and stroke are Light Ivory. Outline the top outer edge of the eye with the silver paint marker. Paint the mouth and nose Charcoal. Add Light Ivory nostrils. Apply the matte spray varnish.

FRIGHTFULLY FUN
FAVORS & GIFTS

TRICK OR TREAT! It's the spookiest night of the year as tricksters of all ages haunt the neighborhood, lurking from house to house to collect their tasty treats. To tempt your little ghosts and gremlins, we invite you to sneak a peek into our secret laboratory where we'll concoct a bevy of ghoulish goodies, fit for any witch or warlock.

Our frightfully fun favors are perfect take-home treats for your monster mash party guests or to hand out to the special neighborhood trick-or-treaters as unique and thoughtful gift ideas. Those little boys and "ghouls" will go "buggy" over our sucker bouquets and delight in taking home their very own creepy candy favor cups. Those leftover lunch bags are the cat's meow when decorated with a scaredy cat motif and filled with spooky sweets.

For more elaborate gift ideas, how about digging into your bag of tricks and whipping up some charming papier mâché candy cups or a mummy coffee can filled with tasty treats for the Halloween hostess? Or use your miniature Halloween cookie cutters to make delightful pin pals to surprise all your graveyard "ghoul-friends." These devilish delights are sure to bring a ghostly grin to young and old alike.

SECTION

2

MUMMY SPOON.................. 28

BLACK CAT
CANDY CUP 30

MUMMY CAN 33

PUMPKIN PIN PAL 34

FRIGHTFULLY FUN
QUICK CRAFTS 36

MUMMY Spoon

For a "spoonful" of spooky fun, craft this charming peek-a-boo mummy to delight your ghostly guests. Fabric stiffener and strips of cheesecloth are all you need to "wrap up" this frightfully fun and easy project. For the perfect party favor, tie a bag of treats to the handle and accent with colorful ribbon trims.

MATERIALS LIST

- paintbrushes and general supplies (see pages 6–7)
- wooden spoon (approximately 11½" [29cm])
- six 12" x 1½" (30cm x 4cm) wide strips of cheesecloth
- fabric stiffener (I use Aleene's Fabric Stiffener and Draping Liquid)
- Delta Ceramcoat acrylic paint: Light Ivory, Charcoal, Quaker Grey, Cardinal Red (for a softer look, use pink powdered blush for the cheeks instead of Cardinal Red)
- Delta Ceramcoat matte interior spray varnish
- 5/16" (8mm) wooden button
- miniature plastic spider
- small cellophane treat bag (with desired treats)
- black cord (or heavy string)
- curling ribbon (I use lime green and purple)
- wax paper
- plastic container or bowl (for fabric stiffener)
- 2" (5cm) foam brush
- old toothbrush
- glue gun and glue sticks
- pattern (page 58)

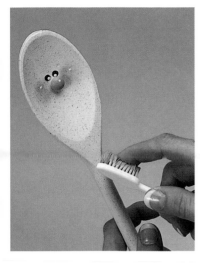  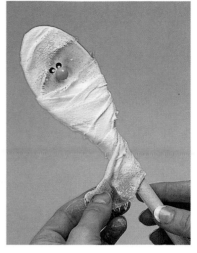

1 Basecoat the spoon with Light Ivory. Freehand the facial features (see pattern on page 58), using Charcoal for the eyes and Light Ivory for the pupils. Drybrush the cheeks with Cardinal Red (or brush on pink powdered blush). Add Light Ivory highlight dots on the cheeks. For the nose, paint a wooden button Quaker Grey, and add a Light Ivory highlight dot. Let dry. Then hot glue the button nose onto the face. Next, spatter the spoon with Quaker Grey and let dry. Apply the matte spray varnish.

2 Cut six strips of cheesecloth approximately 12 " x 1½" (30cm x 4cm) wide. Set the cheesecloth strips on a sheet of wax paper.

Pour some fabric stiffener into a plastic container or bowl. Using the foam brush, moisten the cheesecloth strips with the fabric stiffener.

3 Wrap the moistened strips around the mummy spoon, allowing the facial features to show through. Continue wrapping the strips downward around the handle. Dip the foam brush into the fabric stiffener and apply to any dry pieces of cheesecloth, draping as desired. Allow to dry.

CREATE A FRANKIE SPOON

To create the Frankie Spoon, basecoat a wooden spoon using Delta's Lima Green. Trace or transfer the facial features (see page 58). Paint the hair, eyes, scar and wooden button nose Charcoal. Add Light Ivory pupils and Light Ivory highlights to the hair and nose. Drybrush the cheeks with Cardinal Red and add Light Ivory highlight dots. Hot glue the button nose to the spoon. Spatter the spoon with Charcoal and Light Ivory, then apply the matte varnish. Use a black cord to attach a bag of goodies and accent with curling ribbon.

4 Hot glue a miniature plastic spider onto the mummy spoon. For the treat bag, fill a small cellophane bag with goodies. Tie the top of the bag closed with a piece of cord and then tie the cord around the handle of the spoon. Hot glue pieces of curling ribbon onto the treat bag for a festive touch.

BLACK CAT
Candy Cup

Give your graveyard guests something to take home—besides the shivers! Fashioned from a hollowed-out Styrofoam ball and instant papier mâché, this charming black cat candy cup is far too cute to give anyone a fright. Add a giggling ghost and a perky pumpkin (see page 32) and you've got the perfect trio of spooky pals to celebrate this haunted holiday.

MATERIALS LIST

- paintbrushes and general supplies (see pages 6–7)

- 3" (8cm) Styrofoam ball

- instant papier mâché (I use Celluclay Instant Papier Mâché)

- white acrylic gesso

- Delta Ceramcoat acrylic paint: Charcoal, Lima Green, Light Ivory, Terra Cotta

- Delta Ceramcoat matte interior varnish

- iridescent crystal glitter

- 6" (15cm) piece of 6mm silver tinsel stem

- small candies to fill cup (such as candy corn, M&M's, etc.)

- sharp knife

- mixing bowl

- wax paper

- bowl of warm water

- glue gun and glue sticks

- pattern (page 58)

PROJECT TIP

While working on your project, keep the papier mâché mixture in a bowl covered with wax paper or plastic wrap to prevent dryness. To store the papier mâché, place it in a resealable plastic bag and keep in the refrigerator.

1 Use a sharp knife to cut a small sliver off the bottom of the Styrofoam ball. The ball should sit upright without rolling over.

2 Use a knife to carve out an opening in the top of the Styrofoam ball deep enough to hold your candy treats. Press your thumb into the opening to further indent and smooth out the surface.

3 Mix the papier mâché with warm water following the manufacturer's instructions. (I find it easier to mix the mâché in a mixing bowl rather than in a plastic bag.) Knead the mixture until it is smooth and has the consistency of stiff cookie dough.

Next, cover your work surface with wax paper. Use your fingers to apply the papier mâché mixture onto the Styrofoam ball. Dip your fingers in a bowl of warm water to moisten, then blend the edges until smooth.

4 For the ears, form two ½" (1cm) balls of papier mâché into triangular shapes, then press onto each side of the head. Blend the edges until smooth. Allow to dry.

Next, apply a generous coat of white acrylic gesso to seal the surface of the candy cup.

5 Basecoat the cat Charcoal. To paint the features, simply freehand them or transfer the pattern on page 58 (for details, see Using Patterns & Templates on page 54). Paint the eyes Lima Green with Charcoal pupils and Light Ivory highlights. Paint the eyebrows Light Ivory. Next, paint the nose Terra Cotta and add a Light Ivory highlight dot. For the mouth and whiskers, use Light Ivory. Paint the inside of the ears Terra Cotta with Light Ivory highlight dots.

6 Apply the matte varnish. While the varnish is still wet, sprinkle with iridescent crystal glitter.

7 For the hanger, cut a 6" (15cm) piece of silver tinsel stem. Hot glue the tinsel stem inside the opening. Fill your candy cup with small candies.

CRAZY CANDY CUPS

For the ghost and pumpkin, instead of forming the ears in step 4, form a ³⁄₈" (1cm) ball of papier mâché for each nose. Press the nose onto the center of the face. Blend the edges until smooth. Allow to dry.

Paint the Ghost Light Ivory. Freehand or transfer the facial features (see page 58). Paint the eyes Charcoal with Light Ivory pupils. Paint the eyebrows Charcoal and the nose Terra Cotta with a Light Ivory highlight dot. The mouth is Charcoal with a Terra Cotta tongue. The highlight dot on the tongue is Light Ivory.

Paint the Pumpkin Terra Cotta. Freehand or transfer the facial features (see page 58). Paint the eyes Light Ivory with Charcoal pupils and outlines. Paint the eyebrows and nose Charcoal. Add a Light Ivory highlight dot to the nose. Using Light Ivory, paint the teeth, and then outline them with Charcoal.

MUMMY Can

Recycle those leftover coffee cans into delightfully ghoulish gifts. With some plaster gauze, and a sprinkling of spooky magic, your mummy will come to life to deliver your tasty Halloween tricks and treats. For the perfect finishing touch, wrap your gruesome gifts in cellophane and accent with some festive ribbon trims. Once the gifts have disappeared, the mummy container can store your yummy Halloween treats year after year.

MATERIALS LIST

- paintbrushes and general supplies (see pages 6–7)

- tin coffee can (1 kg size: 6½" high x 6" diameter [17cm x 15cm])

- plaster gauze (I use one standard size 180" x 4" [5m x 10cm] wide roll of Rigid Wrap Plaster Cloth)

- white acrylic gesso

- Delta Ceramcoat acrylic paint: Light Ivory, Quaker Grey, Charcoal, Lima Green, Cardinal Red

- Delta Ceramcoat matte interior spray varnish

- ¾" (2cm) wooden button

- ½" (1cm) orange button

- two 1" (3cm) square fabric patches

- plastic spider

- For inside tin: cellophane, various Halloween-themed toys, treats, favors or party accessories

- black, orange and lime green curling ribbon

- wax paper

- glue gun and glue sticks

- pattern (page 58)

1 Cover your work surface with wax paper. Cut three 21" (53cm) pieces of plaster gauze. Moisten one of the pieces with water. Beginning at the top opening, wrap the moistened piece of plaster gauze around the surface of the can. Continue to moisten and apply the remaining strips, overlapping each piece as you cover the entire surface. Let dry.

2 Next, cut the rest of the plaster gauze into five 22"–23" (56cm–58cm) pieces. One at a time, fold each piece in half lengthwise, then moisten with water. Place each strip around the can at an angle, overlapping as desired. Allow to dry.

3 Apply a generous coat of white acrylic gesso to seal the surface of the can. Apply additional coats as desired. Allow to dry.

4 Basecoat the mummy with Light Ivory. Shade the edges of each strip with a wash of Quaker Grey.

5 Referring to the pattern on page 58, paint the eyes Charcoal with a Lima Green iris and a Charcoal pupil. Add highlight dots and strokes using Light Ivory. For the cheeks, drybrush with Cardinal Red (or brush on pink powdered blush). For a nose, paint the wooden button Quaker Grey and add a Light Ivory highlight dot.

6 Next, hot glue the nose underneath the eyes, and apply the matte spray varnish.

7 Hot glue two fabric patches onto the bottom left side, overlapping them in the center. Hot glue the orange button onto the center of the patches and the spider onto the bottom right side.

8 Line the inside of the can with cellophane and fill with your desired goodies. Accent with curling ribbon.

PUMPKIN Pin Pal

It's so easy to make this jolly pumpkin pin with some rolled-out clay and a miniature cookie cutter. For an extra special touch, you can attach your painted pin onto a handcrafted gift tag or place card. To join your pumpkin pal, add a spooky bat or ghost to your collection.

GHOST AND BAT PIN PALS

The ghost and bat pins are made the same way, using miniature ghost and bat cookie cutters (see patterns on page 59). Basecoat the ghost Light Ivory and the bat Charcoal. For the ghost, paint the eyes Charcoal with Light Ivory pupils. Paint the mouth Charcoal. For the cheeks use a wash of Dark Goldenrod and add Light Ivory highlight dots. Hot glue the "BOO" alphabet beads onto the ghost pin after the varnish is applied. For the bat, paint the eyes Light Ivory with Charcoal pupils. Paint the nose and mouth Terra Cotta. Add the fangs and the lines along the ridges of the wings using Light Ivory. (For a black cat pin, see page 17 for painting instructions.)

MATERIALS LIST

- paintbrushes and general supplies (see pages 6–7)
- air-dry modeling clay (I use Creative Paperclay)
- Delta Ceramcoat acrylic paint: Dark Goldenrod, Dark Forest Green, Light Ivory, Charcoal, Terra Cotta
- Delta Ceramcoat matte interior spray varnish
- miniature pumpkin cookie cutter
- ¾" (2cm) pin back
- wax paper
- rolling pin
- bowl of warm water
- old toothbrush
- glue gun and glue sticks
- pattern (page 59)

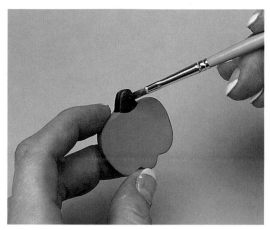

1 Cover your work surface with wax paper. Use the rolling pin to flatten the air-dry modeling clay to ¼" (6mm) thickness. Use a miniature pumpkin cookie cutter to cut out the shape. Remove the excess clay from around the edges of the cookie cutter.

Dip your fingers in a bowl of warm water to moisten, then blend the edges of the pumpkin ornament until smooth. Allow the clay ornament to dry. Be sure to turn it over frequently to facilitate even drying.

2 Basecoat the pumpkin Dark Goldenrod with a Dark Forest Green stem. Freehand or transfer the facial features (see pattern on page 59). (I think it is easier to freehand the features since the clay piece is so small.)

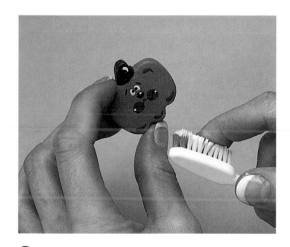

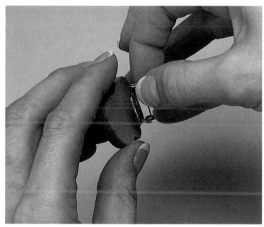

3 Paint the eyes Light Ivory with Charcoal pupils. Paint the eyebrows and nose Charcoal. Add a Light Ivory highlight dot to the nose. Use Terra Cotta for the cheeks and add Light Ivory highlight dots. Paint the mouth Charcoal. Using Terra Cotta, add four highlight strokes on the pumpkin. Using Light Ivory, add one highlight stroke on the stem.

Next, spatter very sparingly with Light Ivory. Apply the matte spray varnish.

4 Hot glue the metal pin clasp onto the back of the ornament.

Make Halloween Button Covers

Your pin pals also make charming button covers. Just glue a metal button clasp instead of a pin clasp onto the back of each ornament.

Scaredy Cat Munchie Mix Bags

MATERIALS: general supplies (see pages 6–7) / tracing paper, transfer paper and lightweight cardboard or posterboard / black craft foam / 10½" x 5" (27cm x 13cm) paper lunch sack / black and orange dimensional paint / Delta Ceramcoat acrylic paint: Dark Goldenrod, Light Ivory, Charcoal / Delta Ceramcoat matte interior spray varnish / two 10mm wiggly eyes / ½" (2cm) orange button / three 5" (13cm) pieces of 6mm silver tinsel stems / one strand of black raffia / small pieces of sponge / one ¾"–1" (2cm–3cm) square piece of sponge / marking pen / ⅛" (3mm) hole punch / old toothbrush / glue gun and glue sticks / pattern (page 59) / munchie mix: prepackaged caramel popcorn with peanuts, Halloween M&M's, candy pumpkins and candy corn

1 Create a template for the cat shape (see pages 54 and 59) and then cut the cat shape out of black foam. **2** Outline the cat shape, left ear and in between the legs with the black dimensional paint. Paint accents on the ears, foot and tail with orange dimensional paint and let dry. Next, hot glue the wiggly eyes and the orange button. Bend a tinsel stem into a spiral and hot glue it onto the center of the cat. **3** Sponge paint the front of the bag with Dark Goldenrod. Then spatter the bag with Charcoal and Light Ivory and let dry. Fold the top of the bag over 2" (5cm). With a square piece of sponge, paint a checkerboard pattern along the top and bottom of the bag, alternating between Charcoal and Light Ivory. Let dry. Using dimensional paint, apply orange dots onto the Charcoal checks and black dots onto the Light Ivory checks and let dry. Apply the matte spray varnish. **4** Hot glue the cat onto the bag. Hot glue a tinsel stem above the bottom and below the top checkerboard trims. Punch two holes in the top center of the bag approximately 1½" (4cm) apart. Place the prepared munchie mix in a sealed plastic bag before placing it inside the decorated bag. Secure the bag with black raffia, threading it through the holes and forming a bow.

Going Buggy Sucker Bouquets

MATERIALS: 2½" (6cm) wide rose pot, 4" (10cm) high / floral foam brick / artificial spider webbing / assorted Halloween suckers and lollipops / orange and black excelsior (or Spanish moss) / gummy worms (optional) / miniature plastic bugs (such as spiders and flies) / sharp knife / glue gun and glue sticks

1 Cut a piece of the floral foam brick to fit inside the clay pot. Then hot glue the foam brick inside the pot. Next, hot glue the spider webbing around the pot. **2** Insert the stems of the suckers and lollipops into the floral foam base. **3** Hot glue the excelsior or Spanish moss around the base of the pot to hide the floral foam. You could also place edible gummy worms around the suckers, which would add to the "bug" theme of the favor pots. For the finishing touch, hot glue the plastic bugs onto the pot.

Frankie Favor Cup

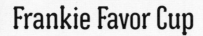

MATERIALS: paintbrushes and general supplies (see pages 6–7) / 3½" x 3¼" (9cm x 8cm) diameter clear plastic drinking cup / Delta Ceramcoat acrylic paint: Lima Green, Charcoal, Light Ivory, Deep Lilac / Delta Ceramcoat matte interior spray varnish / small pieces of sponge / fine-point silver metallic paint marker / pattern (page 59) / favors to fill the cup: assorted treats, miniature toys, Halloween napkin, plasticware

1 Sponge paint the outer surface of the cup using Lima Green and allow to dry. Next, sponge paint the top of the cup with Charcoal for the hair. **2** Trace or freehand the facial features (see pattern on page 59). Paint the eyes Charcoal with Light Ivory pupils and highlights, the nose Deep Lilac with a Light Ivory highlight dot, the mouth and scar Charcoal, and the two teeth Light Ivory outlined with Charcoal. Next, write the desired name at the top of the cup using the metallic paint marker. Apply the matte spray varnish. **3** Fill the favor cup with your desired treats, Halloween napkin, plasticware, miniature toys, etc.

Mr. Whiskers Peat Pot

MATERIALS: paintbrushes and general supplies (see pages 6–7) / tracing paper, transfer paper and lightweight cardboard or posterboard / 3" (8cm) peat pot / black stiffened felt / Delta Ceramcoat acrylic paint: Charcoal / Delta Ceramcoat matte interior spray varnish / 6mm silver tinsel stems: two 7" (18cm) and two 3¾" (10cm) pieces / ½" (1cm) orange button / two 10mm wiggly eyes / 8" (20cm) piece of 15mm black chenille stem / 12" (30cm) piece of 8mm orange and black striped chenille stem / orange and black excelsior / assorted Halloween treats / glue gun and glue sticks / pattern (page 59)

1 Basecoat the peat pot Charcoal. Apply the matte spray varnish. **2** Create a template (see page 54) or freehand the ear pattern (see page 59) onto black stiffened felt twice and cut out. Cut two 3¾" (10cm) pieces of silver tinsel stems and hot glue the stems around the outer edge of the ears. Hot glue the two ears onto the inside front of the pot. **3** Cut two 7" (18cm) pieces of silver tinsel stems. Bend stems and curl edges downward to form whisker shapes. Hot glue the two whisker stems onto the front center of the pot. Next, hot glue the orange button onto the center of the whiskers for the nose. Then, hot glue the two wiggly eyes just above the button nose. **4** For the tail, cut an 8" (20cm) piece of 15mm black chenille stem. Curl the tip of the tail, then hot glue onto the back of the pot. Next, hot glue the 12" (30cm) orange and black striped chenille stem inside the pot for the handle. Fill the pot with excelsior and your favorite treats.

MONSTER MASH

THE LIGHTS ARE LOW...THE PUMPKINS ARE AGLOW...
It's time to celebrate the most frightful night of the year with all sorts of festive fun. And we're pulling out lots of spooky surprises from our bag of treats to help make your next monster mash the most memorable party on the block.

Your ghoulish grown-up guests will be chilled to the bone with our severed finger party favors. Not for the faint of heart, these oh-so-scary body parts are guaranteed to stir up some spine-tingling shrieks and shivers. For the kids, there are oodles of not-so-scary ideas for party fun such as munching on some cookie monster pizza and sharing some ghostly giggles acting out their very own finger puppet shows. They'll delight in dodging some dangling spider guests and picking their favorite treat off a perky pumpkin tree.

And it just wouldn't be a party without brewing up a cauldron full of tempting treats and graveyard goodies that your little ghouls will devour. Tested by our master "kitchen witch," these eerie edibles are so easy to make, you won't even need to borrow her magic spell book.

SECTION

3

PICK-A-TREAT JAR 40

SEVERED FINGERS 42

HAUNTED
GRAVEYARD STAGE.............44

COOKIE MONSTER
PIZZA BOX........................47

MONSTER QUICK CRAFTS 48

TERROR-IFIC TIPS.............50

QUICK & EERIE EDIBLES.......51

Pick A Treat!

PICK-A-TREAT Jar

With a touch of Halloween magic, you can transform an ordinary glass mason jar into an enchanting pumpkin tree. This cheerful chum is sure to be the most popular pumpkin in the patch as he shares his spooky treats with all your merry monsters. And once his treats have disappeared, don't despair— just decorate the branches with your favorite ornament trims for the perfect tabletop treasure.

MATERIALS LIST

- paintbrushes and general supplies (see pages 6–7)

- wide-mouth quart mason jar

- floral foam brick

- spooky Halloween tree (approximately 13" [33cm] long) (or use a dead branch spray-painted black)

- spray primer (or basecoat with acrylic gesso)

- Delta Ceramcoat acrylic paint: Terra Cotta, Dark Goldenrod, Charcoal, Light Ivory, Deep Lilac, Cardinal Red

- Delta Ceramcoat matte interior spray varnish

- ³⁄₄" (2cm) wooden button

- artificial spider webbing

- orange and black excelsior (or Spanish moss)

- various Halloween treats (I use marshmallow ghosts, pumpkin gum balls, candy corn and lollipops)

- small plastic sandwich bags

- curling ribbon (I use purple, orange and white)

- "Pick-A-Treat" tag (optional): white cardstock, ¹⁄₈" (3mm) hole punch, black alphabet stickers or black permanent pen, silver metallic paint marker, decorative edge scissors

- small piece of sponge

- sharp knife

- old toothbrush

- glue gun and glue sticks

- pattern (page 60)

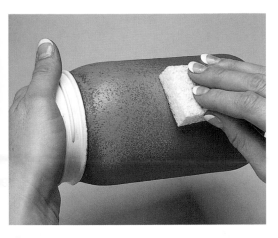

1 Spray the jar with primer or apply a coat of white acrylic gesso. This will enable the paint to adhere to the glass surface of the jar. Next, basecoat the jar with Terra Cotta and let dry. Using a small piece of dampened sponge, apply Dark Goldenrod for a textured effect. Paint the rim of the jar Charcoal.

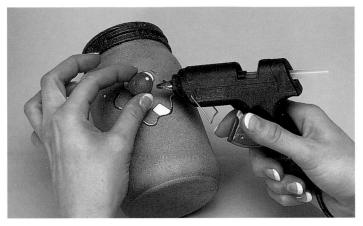

2 Freehand or transfer the facial features (see pattern on page 60). Paint the eyes Light Ivory with Charcoal irises and Light Ivory pupils. Then outline the eyes and paint the eyebrows with Charcoal. For the mouth, use Charcoal with Light Ivory highlight strokes. The tooth is Light Ivory outlined with Charcoal. For the cheeks, drybrush with Cardinal Red and add Light Ivory highlight dots. For the nose, paint a wooden button Deep Lilac and add a Light Ivory highlight dot.

Using an old toothbrush, spatter the jar and button nose with Light Ivory. Apply the matte spray varnish to the jar and button nose. Then hot glue the nose directly underneath the eyes.

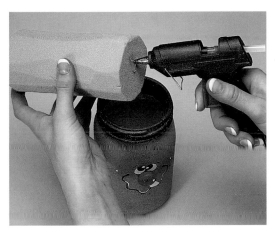

3 Cut the floral foam brick into a cylindrical shape to fit inside the jar. Apply hot glue to the bottom of the brick. Insert the brick into the jar, so the hot glue adheres to the bottom of the jar. Add a generous amount of hot glue around the outer edges of the foam brick to secure to rim.

4 Apply the artificial webbing around the tree's branches. Insert the base of the tree into the foam brick inside the jar. Then remove the tree and add hot glue into the hole in the foam brick. Reinsert the tree and allow to set. Adjust the branches as desired. Hot glue the excelsior around the base of the tree.

5 Decorate the branches with spooky treats. Wrap the treats in clear plastic sandwich bags first, then attach using curling ribbon. Treats that are already wrapped can be attached directly onto the branches with ribbon. Optional: Make a tag using cardstock, decorative scissors, alphabet stickers and a silver paint marker. Punch a hole in one of the top corners and attach the tag to the base of the tree with curling ribbon. Accent the base of the tree with curling ribbon for a festive touch.

SEVERED Fingers

Not for the faint of heart, these frightful finger favors will add some spine-tingling shivers to your ghostly gatherings. But don't get too spooked . . . These gruesome body parts are far from the real thing. Crafted from air-dry clay, they are painted then embellished with realistic blood drippings and some eerie insect critters. For variety, be sure to make some loathsome "lady fingers" by gluing painted fingernails to your creepy collection.

FABULOUS FINGER TIPS

- Be sure to add a severed finger into your Monster Munchie Hand (see page 51) for a real spooky touch.

- Place a severed finger inside a scroll party invitation with the message: "You and all of your body parts are invited to an evening of thrills and chills . . ."

- Place a severed finger on each dinner plate with a name tag attached (like a toe tag from the morgue).

- Place some fingers on your appetizer tray with a sign that says "Finger Food."

- OK, this one is in really bad taste: Pretend you cut your finger with a sharp knife and have a severed finger drop to the floor!

- Create "Lady Fingers" by gluing plastic fingernails onto the tips of the fingers. Use glow-in-the-dark nails or paint them with acrylic paint or nail polish.

MATERIALS LIST

- paintbrushes and general supplies (see pages 6–7)

- air-dry modeling clay (I use Delight air-dry modeling compound, but you could also use Crayola Model Magic in white)

- plastic fingernails

- Delta Ceramcoat acrylic paint: Fleshtone, Tomato Spice, Light Ivory, Spice Brown

- Tulip Slick True Red (or Scribbles Shiny Christmas Red) dimensional paint

- Delta Ceramcoat matte interior spray varnish

- miniature plastic bugs (I use spiders and flies)

- wax paper

- sharp knife

- glue gun and glue sticks

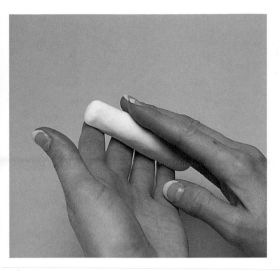

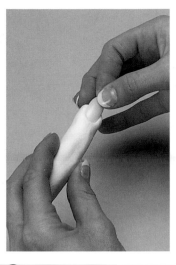

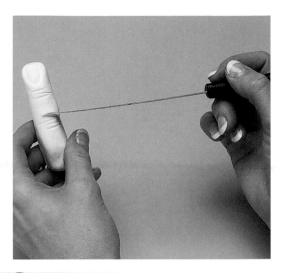

1 Cover your work surface with wax paper. Roll modeling compound into finger shapes of various lengths, approximately 3"–4" (8cm–10cm) long and ³/₄" (2cm) in diameter. Vary the look of your fingers, with some being straight and others being slightly crooked. They will be more interesting if they have irregular shapes.

2 Press a plastic fingernail into the top of the finger to indent a fingernail shape. Remove the fingernail.

3 Gently press a sharp knife into the modeling compound to form ridges on the knuckles and allow to dry. Be sure to turn the fingers over to ensure even drying.

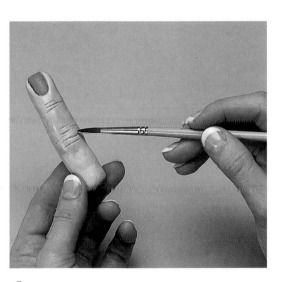

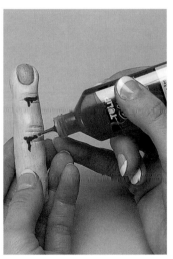

4 Basecoat the fingers Fleshtone. Paint the fingernails with a mixture of Tomato Spice and Light Ivory. Allow to dry.

To antique the fingers, use a wash of Spice Brown. Apply the matte spray varnish.

5 For the look of bloody fingers, apply the red dimensional paint to the desired areas. Allow to dry.

6 You can also hot glue miniature plastic spiders, flies and other bugs onto your fingers.

HAUNTED Graveyard Stage

$\mathfrak{S}$et the "stage" for hours of ghostly giggles at your next gruesome gala. Your little monsters will delight in staging their very own finger puppet shows with this quick and easy graveyard scene. A cardboard gift box is cut, painted and embellished with tombstones, eerie eyes, spooky spiders and other terrifying trims—a perfect backdrop for the ghost finger puppets featured on page 48.

Gruesome Graveyard Fun

Create a gruesome graveyard in your own front yard! Make tombstones out of foamboard, then spray with fleckstone paint for a realistic stone look. Secure them into the ground with wooden stakes. If you are feeling particularly wicked, make your trick-or-treaters walk through your haunted graveyard to get to the treats. For other Terror-ific Tips, see page 50.

MATERIALS LIST

- paintbrushes and general supplies (see pages 6–7)

- tracing paper and transfer paper

- heavy cardboard gift box with lid cut off (approximately 9" high x 12" wide x 2½" deep [23cm x 30cm x 6cm]) (The box can vary in size. Just cut the center opening accordingly.)

- gray stiffened felt

- Delta Ceramcoat acrylic paint: Charcoal, Straw

- Tulip Slick White or Ivory (or Scribbles Shiny White or Shiny Winter White) dimensional paint

- Delta Ceramcoat matte interior spray varnish

- Spanish moss

- desired Halloween trims (I use three miniature raffia pumpkins, two plastic spiders and a miniature plastic bat)

- six 10mm wiggly eyes (or use a variety of sizes for contrast)

- artificial spider webbing

- craft knife (or utility knife)

- old toothbrush

- glue gun and glue sticks

- patterns (page 60)

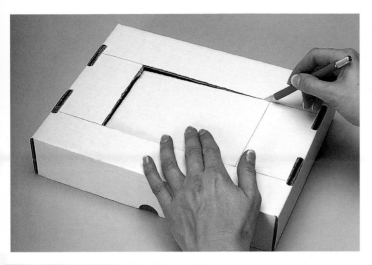

1 Using sharp scissors, cut the lid off the cardboard gift box. Discard the lid. Use a ruler and pencil to sketch the opening of the stage 6¹/₂" wide x 4¹/₂" high (17cm x 11cm) in the approximate center of the box. (I centered my opening along the width but positioned the opening 2" [5cm] from the top and 2¹/₂" [6cm] from the bottom vertically.) Use a craft knife or utility knife to cut out the opening of the stage.

2 Basecoat the cardboard stage with Charcoal. Use an old toothbrush to spatter the box heavily with Straw. This will create the look of stars. When dry, apply the matte spray varnish.

3 To create the tombstones (I use two large and three small tombstones), freehand or transfer the tombstone patterns (see page 60) onto gray stiffened felt. I find it is easier to make a cardboard template of the tombstone, so the shape can be traced more easily onto the stiffened felt (see Creating Templates on page 54). Then cut out the tombstones.

Using the dry-brush technique, apply Charcoal paint around the outer edges of the felt tombstone shapes for added dimension.

4 Use the dimensional paint to add designs (see patterns on page 60) or the letters "RIP" to the tombstones. Allow to dry.

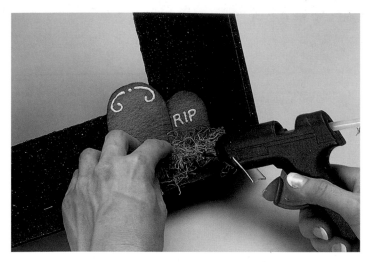

5 Hot glue a large and small tombstone and some Spanish moss onto the right back of the stage. For a three-dimensional effect, cut a small tab out of the stiffened gray felt approximately 2" x $^3/_4$" (5cm x 2cm) wide. Bend the tab in half to form a right angle. (The vertical side of the tab will be glued to the back of the tombstone and the horizontal side will be glued to the bottom of the stage, forming a stand.) Hot glue the vertical side of the tab to the back of the remaining large tombstone at the very bottom. Using the horizontal side of the tab, hot glue the large tombstone closer to the edge of the stage, with the two smaller tombstones glued to each side (the tab on the large tombstone will keep the tombstones standing straight).

Next, hot glue a miniature plastic bat to the top of the large tombstone. Add more Spanish moss around the tombstones as desired. Hot glue the three miniature raffia pumpkins. Glue a miniature plastic spider onto one of the pumpkins. Hot glue the three sets of wiggly eyes onto the back of the stage.

Ghost Finger Puppets

Now that your stage is ready to be haunted, check out the Ghost Finger Puppet on page 48.

6 Hot glue the artificial spider webbing for a real spooky effect. Glue a plastic spider near the top left side of the stage.

COOKIE MONSTER Pizza Box

Your monster mash will be the hit of the block when you serve a sampling of yummy cookie pizza inside this charming painted pizza box (see page 52 for cookie recipe). This goofy-grinned monster loves freshly baked cookies, especially when they're crawling with gruesome gummy worms. For hours of frightful fun, have your little boys and "ghouls" decorate their own cookie pizzas.

MATERIALS LIST

- paintbrushes and general supplies (see pages 6–7)

- 10" (25cm) cardboard pizza box

- Delta Ceramcoat acrylic paint: Lima Green, Charcoal, Light Ivory, Deep Lilac

- Delta Ceramcoat matte interior spray varnish

- plastic spider

- small piece of sponge

- fine-point black permanent marker (such as the Pigma Micron 05 or Zig Memory System 05)

- fine-point silver metallic paint marker

- old toothbrush

- glue gun and glue sticks

- pattern (page 60)

1 Using a piece of dampened sponge, apply Lima Green to the outside surface of the box. Allow to dry.

2 To paint the facial features, freehand or transfer the pattern on page 60. Paint the hair Charcoal. The eyes are Light Ivory with a Charcoal iris and Light Ivory pupils. The highlight dots are Light Ivory. The eyebrows are Charcoal. The nose is Deep Lilac with three Light Ivory highlight dots. Paint the mouth Charcoal and the teeth Light Ivory. The dots on the cheeks are Light Ivory.

3 Outline the eyes, nose and teeth with a fine-point black permanent marker.

4 Using an old toothbrush, spatter the box with Light Ivory.

5 Trace or freehand the lettering. Use a silver paint marker to write "Gimme Cookie!" along the hairline. Apply the matte spray varnish. Hot glue a plastic spider onto the upper left-hand side of the box.

Cookie Monster Pizza

The instructions for making the Cookie Monster Pizza are on page 52. Check out the other Quick & Eerie Edibles on pages 51–53 ... if you dare.

Ghost Finger Puppet

MATERIALS: paintbrushes and general supplies (see pages 6–7) / air-dry modeling clay (I use Delight air-dry modeling compound but you could also use Crayola Model Magic in white) / Delta Ceramcoat acrylic paint: Light Ivory, Charcoal, Cardinal Red (or pink powdered blush) / Delta Ceramcoat matte interior varnish / iridescent crystal glitter / candy sticks or Halloween pencils, curling ribbon (OPTIONAL) / wax paper / pattern (page 61)

1 Cover your work surface with wax paper. Roll the modeling compound into a ball approximately 1¹/₂"–1³/₄" (3.8cm–4.4cm). Insert your finger into the ball, molding the clay around your finger to form a ghost shape. Use your fingers to form folds and indentations. Allow to dry, turning the ghost over to ensure even drying. **2** Basecoat the ghost Light Ivory. Referring to the pattern on page 61, use Charcoal for the eyes, Light Ivory for the pupils and Charcoal for the mouth. For the cheeks, either drybrush with Cardinal Red or brush on pink powdered blush and add Light Ivory highlight dots. **3** Apply the matte varnish. While the varnish is still wet, sprinkle with crystal glitter. Optional: For a Ghost Finger Puppet Favor, place a candy stick inside the ghost and accent with curling ribbon for a festive touch. Or, place a Halloween pencil inside the puppet for a quick and easy pencil topper.

Ghost Messenger Party Invitations

MATERIALS: general supplies (see pages 6-7) / tracing paper, transfer paper and lightweight cardboard or posterboard / glossy white posterboard or cardstock / Tulip Slick White (or Scribbles Shiny White) dimensional paint / pink powdered blush / alphabet letter beads / two heart beads / black elastic cord / ¹/₈" (3mm) hole punch / fine-point silver metallic paint marker / fine-point black permanent marker (such as the Pigma Micron 05 or Zig Memory System 05) / small brush / pattern (page 61)

1 Trace or freehand the ghost shape (see pattern on page 61) onto a piece of lightweight cardboard or posterboard and cut out. Use this cardboard ghost shape as a template to trace the desired number of ghost messengers onto the glossy white posterboard or cardstock (see Creating Templates on page 54). **2** Use the hole punch to insert a hole into each hand. Apply white dimensional paint around the edges of the ghost. Allow to dry. **3** With a black permanent marker, draw the ghost face, using the patterns on page 61 as a reference. When the ink has dried, apply blush for the cheeks. Use the silver metallic paint marker for accents on the side of the head, hand and lower body. **4** String the alphabet beads onto the black cord to spell your desired message. (I use a heart bead to separate each word.) Insert the ends of the cord through the hole in each hand and tie at the back to secure. Write a message or party details using the black permanent marker.

Scary Skull Ornament

MATERIALS: paintbrushes and general supplies (see pages 6–7) / 4" (10cm) papier mâché egg / Delta Ceramcoat acrylic paint: Light Ivory, Charcoal, Lima Green, Cardinal Red (or pink powdered blush) / Delta Ceramcoat matte interior spray varnish / small eye screw / gold cord or thread / pattern (page 61)

1 Basecoat the papier mâché egg Light Ivory. **2** Trace or freehand the facial features (see pattern on page 61). Paint the eyes Charcoal with a Lima Green iris. Paint the pupils Charcoal. Add Light Ivory highlight dots. Paint the nose and mouth Charcoal. For the cheeks, either drybrush with Cardinal Red or brush on pink powdered blush. Apply the matte spray varnish. **3** Attach a small eye screw into the top of the head. For a hanger, cut a piece of gold cord or thread and loop it through the eye screw.

Spooky Spider

MATERIALS: general supplies (see pages 6–7) / tracing paper, transfer paper and lightweight cardboard or posterboard / black stiffened felt (enough for two 3½" [9cm] circles) / 6mm black chenille stems: six 8" (20cm) pieces and two 7" (18cm) pieces / two 20mm wiggly eyes / ½"– ⅝" (1cm–2cm) orange button / 15" (38cm) of 1" (3cm) wide orange plaid wired ribbon / miniature plastic spider / 7"–10" (18cm x 25cm) black nylon craft cord / drawing compass (OPTIONAL) / ⅛" (3mm) hole punch / glue gun and glue sticks / pattern (page 61)

1 Using the pattern on page 61 or a compass, trace or draw two 3½" (9cm) circles onto black stiffened felt and cut out (see Creating Templates on page 54). Place the two felt circles together and punch a hole into the top. **2** Cut six 8" (20cm) and two 7" (18cm) pieces of black chenille stem. On the back side of one of the felt circles (with the hole at top center), hot glue the six 8" (20cm) pieces for the top three legs and the two 7" (18cm) pieces for the bottom legs. Bend the stems downward to shape. **3** Line up the top holes and hot glue the remaining felt circle onto the back side of the spider. Next, hot glue the wiggly eyes and the orange button nose. Form a bow using the ribbon and hot glue it onto the bottom of the spider. Then hot glue a minia-ture plastic spider onto the bow. **4** Knot one end of the nylon cord through the hole in the top of the spider and hot glue at the back to secure. Make a loop at the top for hanging.

Terror-ific Tips

Follow these "terror-ific" tips to turn your home into a haunted house full of spooky surprises!

HAUNTED HIDEAWAYS

HERE ARE SOME GREAT IDEAS FOR HALLOWEEN DECOR:

- To protect your home from blood-thirsty vampires, hang a string of garlic at your front door with a tag that reads "Vampires Keep Out." Accent with red dimensional paint for blood drippings and plastic vampire fangs.

- Create a haunted forest of "dead" trees by gathering old branches and spray painting them black. Place branches in large pots or buckets and decorate the branches with artificial spider webbing and strings of miniature white or orange lights. Hang rubber spiders, ghosts or bats from the branches.

- Create the look of a deserted haunted house by draping white sheets on your furniture, lampshades, etc. Then tilt all the pictures on your walls at an angle so it looks like ghostly spirits are playing silly pranks.

- Decorate your haunted hideaway with creepy monster hands. Although you can purchase many finished varieties at your local novelty or dollar store, you can also make your own by gluing fake fur material onto gardening gloves and gluing monster fingernails onto the fingertips. For witch's hands, use green plastic dishwashing gloves and attach red plastic fingernails and an artificial spider ring. Use green and red dimensional paint for scars and drizzled blood.

- Every haunted house needs a gruesome graveyard. Purchase foam insulation board or foamboard. Cut the foam into the desired shapes, then spray paint with gray or fleckstone. Add dabs of brown and green paint to give your tombstones an aged effect. It's easy to carve jagged "cracks" or lettering into the foam. Secure your foam tombstones into the ground using heavy wire or wooden stakes.

BEASTLY BUFFETS

CREATE A FRIGHTFUL FEAST FOR YOUR HALLOWEEN BUFFET WITH THESE QUICK AND EASY IDEAS. SEE PAGES 51–53 FOR SOME CREEPY RECIPES . . . IF YOU DARE!

- Create a "worm-feast" theme by sprinkling your tablecloth with chocolate cookie crumbs for dirt and placing gummy worms (or rubber worms) everywhere.

- Create a gruesome graveyard scene for your table. Cut gray posterboard in a tombstone shape to write the menu. Use miniature tombstones as place cards for all your guests. Accent the table with moss, spider webbing, ghosts, spooky trees and dry ice for a foggy effect.

- Using white dimensional paint, add spooky spider webs onto an inexpensive black plastic tablecloth. When dry, glue miniature plastic spiders and large wiggly eyes peering out from the webs.

- Miniature plastic rats look great perched on your cheese tray.

- Purchase monster hands at your local party store and use them to hold your napkins and cutlery. Monster hands look great coming out of snack bowls or holding menu boards or party favors.

- Use Halloween cookie cutters to cut spooky shapes from bread, sandwich meats and cheese slices.

- Add a chilling effect to your wine glasses by drizzling the sides with tasty blood drippings. Just use corn syrup that has been colored with red food coloring.

- Set a life-size corpse (handmade of course!) onto one of the chairs to join you and your dinner guests.

- Your party guests will be "frozen" with fear when they spot a gruesome ice hand floating in the punch bowl. Simply fill a plastic disposable glove with cranberry juice (or any red beverage). Tie the top of the glove to secure, then freeze. Carefully peel away the edges of the glove and place your chilling body part in your favorite witch's brew.

- Your graveyard guests will go "buggy" when they see some creepy-crawly ice cubes floating in their beverage. Just freeze small candy bugs, raisins, or gummy worms into an ice cube tray full of water or a colored beverage. Substitute an olive or peeled grape for a frightful frozen eye cube.

Quick & EERIE Edibles

Creepy Caramel Apples

1. Remove stems from apples, then wash and dry.

2. Insert a jumbo craft stick into the top (stem end) of each apple. Place apples on a sheet of wax paper.

3. Chop desired nuts and place in a shallow bowl. Set aside.

4. In a saucepan, stir the caramels and water on low to medium heat until caramels are completely melted.

5. Dip the apples into the melted caramel mixture, spooning the caramel evenly over the surface of the apples.

6. Dip the bottoms of the caramel apples into the chopped nuts and place on a sheet of wax paper. Let set for about 20–30 minutes or until firm.

7. Draw spooky spiders on the apples with black decorating gel and use white gel for the spider's eyes. Or drizzle the apples using red decorating gel for blood drippings.

Materials jumbo craft sticks / wax paper

Ingredients 8 medium-size apples • chopped nuts (I use walnuts) • 21 oz. (or about 75) unwrapped vanilla caramels • 3 tablespoons water • tubes of black and white (for spiders) and/or red (for blood drippings) decorating gel

---

Monster Munchie Hand

1. Follow the instructions on page 43 to make one severed finger.
2. Insert the severed finger into the ring finger of the glove.
3. Mix the munchie ingredients and candy together, then scoop the mix into the glove.
4. Secure the top of the glove with heavy string or twine.
5. Add curling ribbon to conceal the string or twine.
6. **OPTIONAL:** Attach a plastic bug to the glove using a permanent adhesive, such as Fabri-Tac.

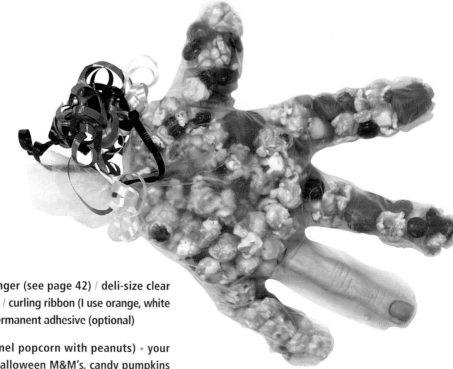

Materials materials to make one severed finger (see page 42) / deli-size clear plastic glove / heavy string or twine / curling ribbon (I use orange, white and black) / large plastic bug and permanent adhesive (optional)

Ingredients munchie mix (prepackaged caramel popcorn with peanuts) • your favorite Halloween candy (I use Halloween M&M's, candy pumpkins and candy corn)

Quick & EERIE Edibles

Scaredy Cat Cupcakes

1. Place paper liners in muffin cups.

2. Prepare cake mix according to instructions on the box.

3. Fill each lined cup with the cake batter and bake until golden brown according to the baking instructions on the box.

4. Allow the cupcakes to cool completely.

5. Spread black icing onto the cupcakes.

6. Add black sugar sprinkles.

7. For the ears, press two candy corns into the icing on the top of the head.

8. Insert an orange M&M for the nose.

9. Use the white decorating gel to make two dots for the eyes.

10. Use a sharp knife to cut six pieces of black shoestring licorice into strips approximately 1¼"–1½" (3cm x 4cm) long. Insert three licorice stems onto each side of the face for whiskers.

Materials muffin baking tins / paper cupcake liners (look for Halloween designs) / sharp knife

Ingredients cake mix (and required ingredients listed on box) • black icing • black sugar sprinkles • candy corn • orange M&M's • black shoestring licorice • white decorating gel

---

Cookie Monster Pizza

1. Flatten one half of the cookie dough onto the round pizza pan.*

2. Bake the cookie according to the package directions or until golden brown. Then allow the cookie to cool.

3. To decorate, drizzle the cookie with white, orange and black decorating gels.

4. Cut the cherries and walnuts, then sprinkle onto the cookie.

5. Add M&M's and Halloween candy sprinkles onto the cookie.

6. Top with gummy worms (I use three).

7. If using the Cookie Monster Pizza Box on page 47, cut a piece of wax paper to fit inside the box. Set the cookie on the wax paper.

8. **OPTIONAL:** Add three plastic spiders around the cookie for a spooky effect. (The plastic spiders may not be suitable for young children.)

Each 510g package makes two cookie pizzas. Use only ½ of the cookie dough for a small cookie pizza that will fit inside the Cookie Monster Pizza Box on page 47.

Materials 12" (30cm) round pizza pan / sharp knife / wax paper / three plastic spiders (optional)

Ingredients refrigerated cookie dough (I use chocolate chip) • decorating gels (I use white, black and orange) • 5–6 finely chopped cherries • chopped walnuts (just enough to sprinkle on top of the pizza) • Halloween M&M's • Halloween candy sprinkles • gummy worms

Crispy Corn Mummy Balls

1. Mix the rice crisp cereal and candy corn in a large mixing bowl. Set aside.

2. In a large saucepan, melt the butter and peanut butter. Add the miniature marshmallows and stir the mixture until it is completely melted.

3. Pour the melted marshmallow mixture over the cereal and candy corn and stir until coated. Roll the crispy corn mixture into balls, then insert a large craft stick into the bottom center of each ball. Let set.

4. Cut a 12" (30cm) square piece of clear cellophane for each ball. Wrap the balls with the cellophane and secure with orange or black curling ribbon.

5. Cut strips of cheesecloth approximately 36" x 2¹/₂" (91cm x 6cm) wide. Fold in half across the length of the strips. Wrap a strip around each mummy ball, securing with hot glue. Leave a small area unwrapped to glue the eyes.

6. Hot glue two wiggly eyes onto the small unwrapped section. Hot glue a miniature plastic spider onto the mummy's head.

7. Cut a 12" (30cm) piece of ribbon and tie a bow. Trim the ends of the bow to the desired length. Hot glue the bow onto the craft stick by the mummy's neck. Then hot glue a black or orange button onto the center of the fabric bow.

Materials

jumbo crafts sticks / clear cellophane (12" square piece for each ball) / orange or black curling ribbon / strips of cheesecloth (approximately 36" x 2¹/₂" [91cm x 6cm] wide, folded in half lengthwise) / 10mm wiggly eyes (two for each mummy ball) / miniature plastic spiders / 12" (30cm) piece of 1" (3cm) wide orange and black plaid ribbon for bow / ¹/₂"–⁵/₈" (1cm–2cm) black or orange buttons / glue gun and glue sticks

Ingredients

4 cups (946ml) rice crisp cereal • 2 cups (473ml) candy corn • ¹/₂ cup (118ml) butter • ¹/₄ cup (60ml) peanut butter • 4 cups (946ml) miniature marshmallows

Ingredients make approximately 8 large crispy corn balls

Yummy Bat Droppings

1. Fill bag with chocolate-covered candies. Secure top of bag with orange curling ribbon.

2. For a decorative tag, use a black permanent marker to print "Yummy Bat Droppings" onto white cardstock. (If you have a computer and printer, you can use a spooky font and then print it out.) Trim the cardstock with decorative scissors. Punch a hole, then tie the tag onto the bag using orange curling ribbon.

3. Hot glue a 6" (15cm) piece of chenille stem onto the back of the plastic bat favor for a hanger.

4. Place the bat ornament favor around the top of the bag.

Materials

small cellophane bags / orange curling ribbon / white cardstock / decorative scissors / black permanent marker / hole punch / 6" (15cm) piece of orange and black 8mm chenille stem / plastic bat party favors / glue gun and glue sticks

Ingredients

chocolate-covered peanuts, almonds or raisins

Using Patterns & Templates

The project patterns are featured on pages 55–61. These patterns can be either transferred using tracing and transfer paper or traced freehand using the pattern as a visual reference.

Transferring Patterns

Use a pencil to trace the desired pattern onto a sheet of transparent tracing paper. Insert a piece of gray transfer paper in between the traced pattern and your surface area. Using a pencil or ballpoint pen, retrace the pattern, transferring it to your surface. Since the transfer paper is coated on one side only, be sure the correct side is facing down by making a small mark to test. To make transferring easier, use masking tape to secure the tracing and transfer paper.

Painting Details

You can use the above technique to transfer the finer details of your projects. Just remember to basecoat all areas first. For the simpler projects, instead of transferring the finer details using the tracing and transfer paper method, freehand them with a pencil using the pattern or finished project as a visual reference.

NOTE: Do not transfer the cheek areas. They were drawn on the patterns simply for visual reference only. Since the cheeks are softly drybrushed, it may be difficult to cover the line left if the cheek area is transferred or sketched.

Creating Templates

When making any of the kraft paper projects, such as the Ghost Decoration (see page 12) or the Jingle Bell Pumpkin (see page 18), I find it easier to create a permanent template first. Instead of transferring each shape directly onto the kraft paper, transfer the shape onto a piece of lightweight cardboard or posterboard to make a cardboard template. You can use this template over and over again by simply tracing around the outer edges with a pencil. This technique will save you oodles of time, especially if you plan to make several projects requiring the same basic shape. For example, using a template is a quick and easy way to make your Ghost Messenger Party Invitations featured on page 48.

This technique is also used to transfer shapes onto the pieces of stiffened felt (see Spooky Spider on page 49 and the tombstones for the Haunted Graveyard Stage on page 44) and onto the craft foam (see Scaredy Cat Munchie Mix Bags on page 36).

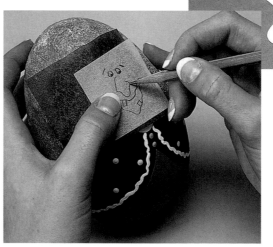

CREATING TEMPLATES
To create a template, trace the pattern onto a piece of cardboard or posterboard, then cut out with scissors. This is a great time-saver when you want to make more than one of the same project.

TRANSFERRING PATTERNS
Use tracing and transfer paper to copy the pattern onto your surface area.

TRANSFERRING PATTERN DETAILS
To transfer details onto irregular shapes, cut the pattern to its actual size rather than working with a full size sheet of tracing paper. You could also freehand the facial features with a pencil, using the pattern as a reference.

Patterns

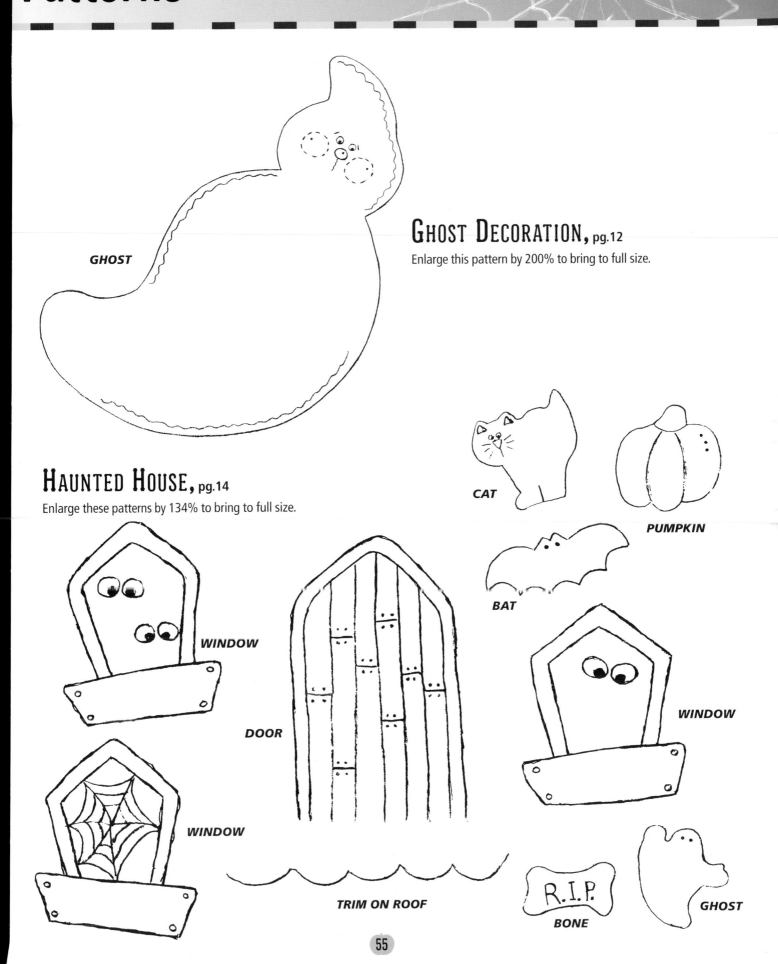

GHOST

GHOST DECORATION, pg.12
Enlarge this pattern by 200% to bring to full size.

HAUNTED HOUSE, pg.14
Enlarge these patterns by 134% to bring to full size.

CAT

PUMPKIN

BAT

WINDOW

DOOR

WINDOW

WINDOW

TRIM ON ROOF

BONE

GHOST

Patterns

JINGLE BELL PUMPKIN, pg.18

Enlarge this pattern by 200% to bring to full size.

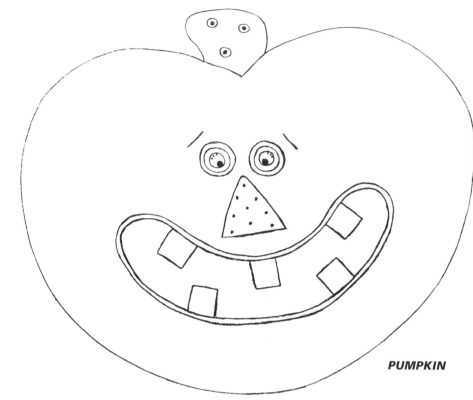

PUMPKIN

SCARED STIFF GHOST TOPIARY, pg. 20

These patterns are full size.

TOPIARY POT

GHOST FACE

BROOM HILDA, pg. 24

This pattern is full size.

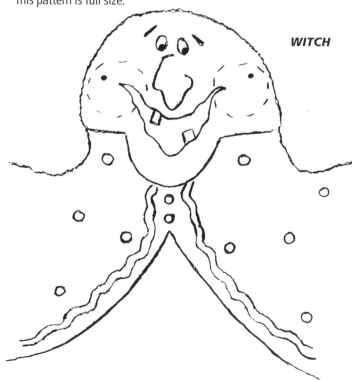

WITCH

GHOST GIFT BAG, pg. 24

Enlarge this pattern by 200%, then enlarge again at 114% to bring to full size.

GHOST

FLUTTERING FRIEND, pg. 25

Enlarge these patterns by 125% to bring to full size.

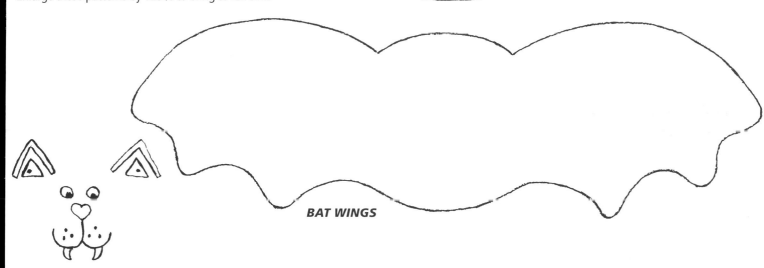

BAT WINGS

BAT FACE

MR. BONES POT, pg. 25

Enlarge these patterns by 125% to bring to full size.

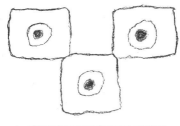

SKULL FACE

CHECKERBOARD TRIM

MUMMY SPOON, pg. 28

Enlarge these patterns by 143% to bring to full size.

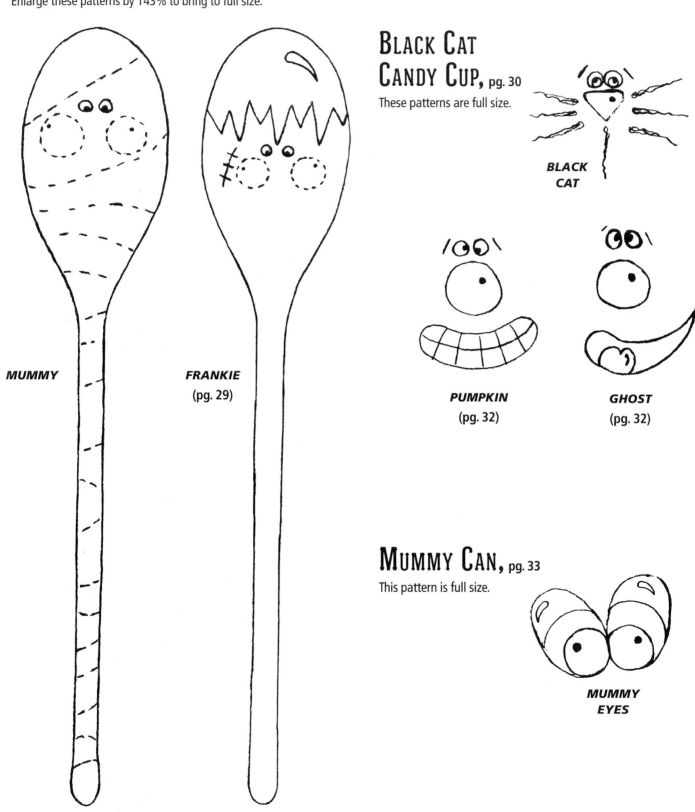

MUMMY

FRANKIE
(pg. 29)

BLACK CAT CANDY CUP, pg. 30

These patterns are full size.

BLACK CAT

PUMPKIN
(pg. 32)

GHOST
(pg. 32)

MUMMY CAN, pg. 33

This pattern is full size.

MUMMY EYES

Pumpkin Pin Pal, pg. 34

These patterns are full size.

PUMPKIN

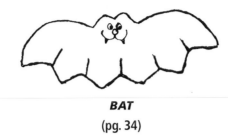

BAT

(pg. 34)

GHOST

(pg. 34)

Scaredy Cat Munchie Mix Bags, pg. 36

This pattern is full size.

Frankie Favor Cup, pg. 37

This pattern is full size.

FRANKIE FACE

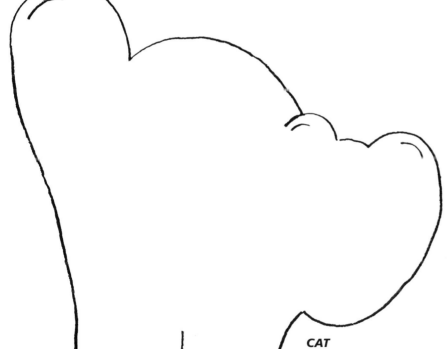

CAT

Mr. Whiskers Peat Pot, pg. 37

This pattern is full size.

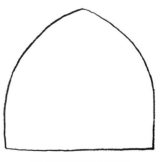

BLACK CAT EAR

Patterns

PICK-A-TREAT JAR, pg. 40

This pattern is full size.

PUMPKIN FACE

HAUNTED GRAVEYARD STAGE, pg. 44

These patterns are full size.

TOMBSTONES

COOKIE MONSTER PIZZA BOX, pg. 47

Enlarge this pattern by 200% to bring to full size.

MONSTER

GHOST FINGER PUPPET, pg. 48

This pattern is full size.

GHOST FACE

GHOST MESSENGER PARTY INVITATIONS, pg. 48

Enlarge these patterns by 134% to bring to full size.

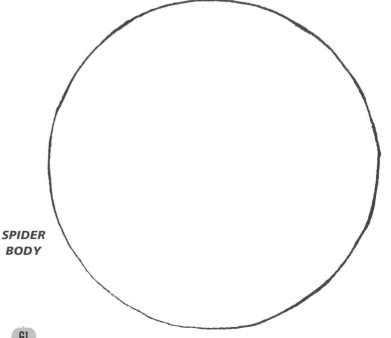

GHOSTS

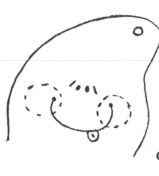

SCARY SKULL ORNAMENT, pg. 49

This pattern is full size.

SKULL FACE

SPOOKY SPIDER, pg. 49

This pattern is full size.

SPIDER BODY

Resources

Activa Products, Inc.
512 So. Garrett
Marshall, TX 75670
(903) 938-2224
www.activa-products.com

• Rigid Wrap Plaster Cloth and Celluclay Instant Papier Mâché

Creative Paperclay Company, Inc.
79 Daily Dr., Ste. 101
Camarillo, CA 93010
(805) 484-6648
www.paperclay.com

• Creative Paperclay and Delight air-dry modeling compound

Delta Technical Coatings, Inc.
2550 Pellissier Pl.
Whittier, CA 90601
(800) 423-4135
www.deltacrafts.com

• Delta Ceramcoat acrylic paints, matte interior and spray varnishes, gesso and general painting supplies

Duncan Enterprises, Inc.
5673 E. Shields Ave.
Fresno, CA 93727
(800) 438-6226 or (559) 291-4444
E-mail: consumer@duncanmail.com
www.duncancrafts.com

• Tulip and Scribbles Dimensional Paints and Aleene's Fabric Stiffener and Draping Liquid

Loew-Cornell, Inc.
563 Chestnut Ave.
Teaneck, NJ 07666-2491
(201) 836-7070
E-mail: loew-cornell@loew-cornell.com
www.loew-cornell.com

• paintbrushes and general painting supplies

Index

Air-dry modeling clays, 7

Bag
   ghost, 24
   munchie mix, 36
Basecoating, 8-9
Bat, 25
Black cat
   candy cup, 30-32
   pot, 37
Box
   pizza, 47
   for puppet stage, 45-46
Brushes, 6
Button covers, 35

Can, coffee, 33
Candy cup, 30-32
Caramel apples, 51
Cheesecloth, 21-22, 29
Chocolate-covered candies, 53
Clay, 7
   blending edges, 16, 35
   severed fingers, 42-43
   tips for working with, 7
Clothespins, using and removing, 22
Cookie pizza, 52
Corn balls, 53
Cup, favor, 37
Cupcakes, 52

Dots, 8-9
Dowel, 22
Drybrushing, 8

Fabric stiffener, 22
Face, painting
   black cat, 31
   friendly monster, 47
   ghost, 13, 23
   mummy, 33
   pumpkin, 19, 41
   witch, 24

Fiberfill, 13, 19
Finger puppet, 48
Fingers, severed, 42-43
Floral foam brick, 36, 41
Fly specking. See Spattering
Food, grotesque, 50

Ghost
   candy cup, 32
   decoration, 12-13
   finger puppet, 48
   gift bag, 24
   party invitations, 48
   topiary, 20-23
Gift bag, ghost, 24
Glass surface, preparing, 41
Graveyard, 44-46

Halloween décor, ideas, 50
Haunted house, 14-17
Highlights, 8-9

Invitations, ghost, 48

Jack-o'-lantern. See Pumpkin
Jar, 40-41

Loew-Cornell brushes, 6

Milk carton, 15
Mummy
   can, 33
   spoon, 28-29
Munchie hand, 51

Painting
   details, 54
   sponge, 9, 21
   supplies, 6
   tips for, 9

Papier mâché
   egg, 24-25
   instant, 7
   mixing, 31
   using and storing, 30
Party food, grotesque, 50
Patterns, 55-61
   transferring, 7
   using, 54
Pins, 34-35
Plaster gauze, 7
Pots, 25, 36-37
Pumpkin, 18-19
   candy cup, 32
   pin, 34-35

Recipes, 51-53

Skull, 49
Spattering, 8-9, 17, 19, 41
Spider, 49
Sponge painting, 9, 21
Spoon, mummy, 28-29
Stage, graveyard, 44-46
Stippling, 8-9, 24
Stone texture, creating, 21
Sucker bouquet, 36
Supplies, 6

Templates, 54
Texturizing
   stone effect, 21
   using sponge painting, 9, 41
Tombstones, 45
Toothbrush, spattering with, 17, 19, 41
Topiary, 20-23
Transferring patterns, 54
Tree, pumpkin, 40-41

Washes, 8
Wire, curling, 13
Witch, 24

More great craft titles from North Light Books!

Create classic holiday decorations that everyone will love! You'll find 13 simple painting projects inside, from Santa figures and Christmas card holders to tree ornaments and candy dishes. Each one includes easy-to-follow instructions, step-by-step photographs and simple designs that you can use on candles, fabric, glass and more.

ISBN 1-58180-237-4, paperback, 112 pages, #32012-K

Discover new tricks for creating extra-special greeting cards with MaryJo McGraw! Pick up your stamps, follow along with the illustrated, step-by-step directions inside, and ta da! You'll amaze everyone—including yourself—with your beautiful and original creations.

ISBN 0-89134-979-0, paperback, 128 pages, #31521-K

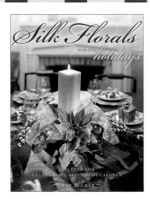

Make your holidays brighter and more special by creating your very own floral décor! Cele Kahle shows you how to create a variety of gorgeous arrangements, swags, topiaries, wreaths and more. You'll create 19 projects in all, using silk foliage, berries, fruit and ribbon. Each one comes with step-by-step guidelines and beautiful full-color photos.

ISBN 1-58180-259-5, paperback, 128 pages, #32124-K

Celebrate and pamper your beloved pets! Pet Crafts features over 28 fun projects for the whole family including dog and cat toys, pet accessories, crafts for kids and pet celebrations. Each project uses simple items easily found in craft stores with safety being a top priority. Both discerning canines and finicky felines are sure to be delighted!

ISBN 1-58180-503-9, paperback, 96 pages, #32847-K

These books and other fine North Light titles are available from your local art & craft retailer, bookstore, online supplier or by calling 1-800-448-0915.